Practice in the Use of English

Also by John Millington Ward

The Use of Tenses in English

Peculiarities in English Grammar

British And American English Books One and Two

The New Intermediate English Course
 Students' Books One and Two
 Teacher's Books One and Two

New Intermediate English Grammar

Practice in Structure and Usage

Proficiency in the Use of English

Fifty Exercises For Practice In Structure and Usage

Practice in the Use of English

100 Exercises

John Millington Ward

Director of the Ward Academy of English Studies
and former Professor of English
in the Royal Hellenic Naval Academy

Longman

Longman Group Limited
Longman House
Burnt Mill, Harlow, Essex CM20 2JE, England
and Associated Companies throughout the world.

First published *1966
New impressions *1967; *1968 (twice);
*1969; *1970 (thrice); *1973; *1974; *1975;
*1976; †1977; †1978; †1980; †1983

ISBN 0 582 52191 2

Acknowledgements
We are indebted to the following for permission to reproduce
copyright material:
Messrs Arthur Guinness Son and Co (Park Royal) Ltd for their
advertising poster, *'What the Situation Demands'*, and the University
of Cambridge Local Examinations Syndicate for material from past
Cambridge Proficiency Examination Papers.
N.B.   In certain instances passages from the Cambridge Proficiency
       Examination papers have been lengthened or shortened and
       in the exercises there are sometimes additions by John
       Millington Ward.

Illustrated by Michael ffolkes

Printed in Singapore by
Kyodo-Shing Loong Printing Industries Pte Ltd.

A few words about this book

The order of these 100 exercises has been arranged with an eye to variety and interest, not to classification of type or grading of difficulty.

John Millington Ward

One

. . . an appetising smell

In the following 25 sentences, fill the blank spaces with the needed adverb-particles (i.e. words like *up*, *down*, *off*, *out*, *in*, *for*, *with*, etc.).

Example: 'I'm going to brush ...... my English a bit.'
Answer: 'I'm going to brush *up* my English a bit.'

1. Are you going to the station to see them ......?
2. The poor chap was attacked by hooligans and cruelly beaten ......
3. The pan on the stove was giving ...... an appetising smell.
4. As they retreated, the enemy blew ...... all the bridges.
5. Look! That aircraft is about to take ......
6. The book is reprinting now. It sold ...... its first edition within a fortnight of publication.
7. Daddy really blew ...... this morning! I've never seen him so angry before.
8. There's something wrong with the car. I've asked the mechanic to see ...... it as soon as possible.
9. I hate insinuations of this sort, Tom. What exactly are you driving ......?
10. No, I haven't met Henry Armstrong yet, but I know ...... him, of course. He's very well known.
11. The car drew ...... in front of the hotel.
12. We begged them to be a bit quieter but they went ...... making the devil of a noise.
13. Poor Peter! In the middle of his party he ran ...... of whisky and there was nobody whom he could ask to run out to get some more.
14. No thanks, I don't smoke. I gave it ...... last year.
15. I'm ringing you to say that my wife is ill and we have to put ......
    our dinner party tomorrow night.
16. He speaks English well, doesn't he? And yet he's never had a lesson. He's picked it ...... himself.
17. Have you settled ...... yet in your new flat?
18. Please send ...... a doctor at once!

1

19. He should be in his office at nine o'clock but he rarely turns ...... much before nine-thirty.
20. She stood for a moment, studying her shopping-list and crossing ...... the things she had already bought.
21. Peter kicked the log in the grate. It broke ...... flame at once.
22. We haven't a spare bed but we can put you ...... on the divan in the living-room.
23. He mumbles so much that I can rarely make ...... what he is saying.
24. The weather forecast said it would be cold and rainy but it turned ...... to be a beautiful day.
25. I refuse to have anything more to do ...... him.

Two

A. In each of these ten sentences, the position of the word *only* produces an unambiguous meaning. Say what this meaning is.

1. I don't know why he's making such a fuss. I only smacked him.
2. We're very fond of that only son of theirs.
3. The Judge was very lenient, not sending him to prison. Only, the fine was pretty stiff.
4. You are the only girl in his life, you know.
5. Why do you only giggle when I ask you a question?
6. She was attractive only in her thirties.
7. What are you getting so angry about? I only kissed your wife's cheek.
8. If only I could buy a car like that!
9. Only by long and hard practice can you hope to become a good pianist.
10. Jim hasn't left yet. I saw him only a few minutes ago.

B. In each of these ten sentences, the word *just* produces an unambiguous meaning. Say what this meaning is.

1. They live just round the corner from here.
2. I've just come to tell you that I can't after all buy your car at the price you're asking.
3. He's just told me that he can't buy the car after all.
4. Better not go in to him just yet. He's still in a foul temper.
5. I just can't understand how you came to do such a stupid thing.
6. If we're careful, we shall have just enough money to see us through for the rest of the month.
7. Mary has just had a baby.
8. Pity you didn't wait a moment longer. He arrived just as you turned the corner.
9. I think that was a very just decision, don't you?
10. Oh good, you've brought my luggage. Just put it down here in the hall, will you, please?

Three

In each of these 25 sentences, a phrase with the word *hand* is missing. Following each sentence are four such phrases but only one can be used in the sentence. Choose this one.

Example: 'I'll send you the book tomorrow ....'
at hand   in hand   by hand   on hand
Answer: 'I'll send you the book tomorrow *by hand*.'

1. We have a bit of money ...... this month, my dear. Go ahead and buy those curtains you want.
   by hand   in hand   to hand   out of hand

2. I'm very angry with him. His manner to me was insultingly ......, I thought.
   off hand   out of hand   in hand   on hand

3. Your repair was put ...... at midday yesterday. It ought to be finished by tomorrow night.
   to hand   in hand   on hand   by hand

4. Dick asked Helen last night to marry him, but she refused him ......, I'm sorry to say.
   by hand   to hand   out of hand   off hand

5. One of these days, somebody will have to take that child very firmly ....
   to hand   in hand   on hand   out of hand

6. Tom likes to have three well-sharpened pencils and a clean india-rubber always ....
   off hand   by hand   to hand   out of hand

7. To our great surprise, we had about fifteen pounds ...... at the end of our holiday.
   in hand   on hand   out of hand   off hand

8. You'll have to be quite strict with little Bobby. He very quickly gets ....
   on hand   in hand   out of hand   by hand

9. We're lucky. We live in a quiet, pretty street, and yet all the necessary shops are close ....
   by hand   in hand   at hand   on hand

10. You're asking when we were last in Paris? Oh dear, I can't remember ....
    off hand   in hand   out of hand   to hand

11. I simply can't take you to the cinema tonight. I have a mountain of work ....
    in hand   on hand   to hand   by hand

12. They have so many orders ...... that they're going to start putting us on overtime.
to hand   in hand   by hand   off hand

13. In a modern kitchen everything is arranged so that all the things we need are conveniently ....
to hand   in hand   by hand   out of hand

14. No, it didn't come by post. It came ....
in hand   by hand   to hand   off hand

15. When the car backfired, my horse got completely ...... and threw me into the ditch!
off hand   out of hand   in hand   by hand

16. I'll have to keep a gun ...... if you say there is a danger that we'll be attacked again tonight.
to hand   off hand   by hand   out of hand

17. He'll have to leave us soon. He has a number of important appointments ....
in hand   on hand   by hand   to hand

18. I went to him hat ...... and begged for my job back, but he just showed me the door.
in hand   to hand   out of hand   off hand

19. There's a little hotel somewhere here ...... that I stayed at some years ago.
by hand   at hand   in hand   off hand

20. I'll have to look in the dictionary because I can't remember the word ....
out of hand   at hand   by hand   off hand

21. Yes, I know it's expensive, but it's worth it. It is made ....
from hand   in hand   out of hand   by hand

22. The letter was passed ...... to hand and read by everybody present.
by hand   from hand   in hand   out of hand

23. Please, do let me have it as soon as possible. Send it ......, will you?
in hand   by hand   to hand   on hand

24. The ear-rings that are made in this village are still made entirely ....
out of hand   by hand   to hand   in hand

25. Jenkins may be an excellent scholar, but he can't keep his pupils ....
in hand   on hand   to hand   out of hand

Four

Say what each of these 20 things is used for by answering the imaginary
question 'What's a _____ for?' or 'What are _____s for?'

*Each of your answers should begin with 'It's' or 'They're', each should
use an infinitive, and each should end with a preposition.*

Example: A raincoat (*'What's a raincoat for?'*)
Answer: It's to keep dry in.
     (or) It's to keep the rain off.

1. a carpet
2. a walking-stick
3. a razor
4. a well
5. pavements
6. wash-basins
7. a diving board
8. a vacuum cleaner
9. a glass
10. a mirror
11. a dictionary
12. a divan
13. windows
14. a bedside light
15. a kitchen sink
16. a shower
17. a desk
18. bandages
19. an umbrella
20. fires

Five

That silly fellow didn't understand . . .

In each of the 25 sentences below that are marked *b.* say which word
carries the principal stress. (Ignore the words that are shown in
parentheses.)

Example: a. 'I can't find my umbrella anywhere. Have you seen it?'
        b. 'It's in the car.'
Answer: b. 'It's in the *car.*'
        (i.e. the stress is on the word *car.*)

1a. We spent a couple of weeks in Corfu last year.
  b. So did we.

2a. We were there in summer, and it was so hot!
  b. (Was it?) Do you like it so hot?

3a. Look, you've got some lipstick on your nose.
  b. (Well, well.) So I have!

4a. Have you done that job?
  b. (No, but don't worry.) I'm going to do it.

5a. Did you see her on your way to the office?
  b. (No.) I saw her on my way from the office.

6a. Thank you so much for all you've done.
  b. Thank you, too.

7a. That silly fellow didn't understand what I said.
  b. Nor did anybody.

8a. Did you say you'd go for a paper?
  b. (No.) I said I wanted you to go for a paper.

9a. Let's have another bottle.
  b. But it costs a pound.

10a. Where's your composition, Mary?
  b. I haven't written one.

11a. I adore you.
  b. I adore you.

12a. Did you go there yesterday?
  b. (No.) I'm going there tonight.

13a. When do you leave?
  b. I'm not going, after all.

14a. Which is your hat?
  b. (I can't see it.) But this is my umbrella.

15a. Where's Jimmy?
  b. I don't know. His father's looking for him, too.

16a. Who's in the bathroom?
  b. Who do you think?

17a. Is he studying English?
  b. (Yes.) And he's studying it more seriously than I have ever done.

18a. What's he doing now?
  b. How on earth should I know?

19a. Did you like his idea?
  b. (Well,) I liked hers better.

20a. Why on earth should we hurry?
  b. But they are waiting for us.

21a. When does your ship sail?
  b. I'm going by air after all.

22a. Did you say he was a prince of story-tellers?
  b. (No.) I said he was the prince of story-tellers.

23a. Roses were twelve and a half pence a bunch yesterday.
  b. I know, and they're seventeen and a half pence today.

24a. That was a wonderful dish.
  b. Except for the pepper, I agree with you.

25a. That man a relation of ours? Nonsense!
  b. I tell you he is a relation of ours.

Six

These pairs of words frequently occur together in English, joined by *and*. Say which is the order in which they are generally used. Then put them into sentences that will illustrate their meanings or uses.

Example: seek
hide

Answer: hide and seek

Sentence: The children are playing hide and seek in the garden.

1. goods
chattels

2. figures
facts

3. high-water
hell

4. collar
tie

5. ink
pen

6. sticks
stones

7. thunder
blood

8. ladies
gentlemen

9. women
men

10. women
children

11. to
fro

12. tooth
nail

13. drakes
ducks

14. odds
ends

15. sick
tired

16. rules
regulations

17. needles
pins

18. waifs
strays

19. simple
pure

20. bits
pieces

Seven

Here are 25 pairs of sentences which are identical except for a slight change of wording, a change in the order of the words, or a change in the punctuation. Say how these changes alter the meanings.

1a. They'd arrive early, before anyone else.
 b. They'd arrived early, before anyone else.

2a. It's already midnight. I don't particularly want to go to another nightclub.
 b. It's already midnight. I particularly don't want to go to another nightclub.

3a. Sam planned to murder his boss.
 b. Sam planned the murder of his boss.

4a. The sheep which had not been brought under cover were killed by the sub-zero temperatures.
 b. The sheep, which had not been brought under cover, were killed by the sub-zero temperatures.

5a. I wonder why you bought such an enormous car.
 b. I wonder that you bought such an enormous car.

6a. The twins, Helen and Pauline, were the only ones who didn't pass the examination.
 b. The twins, Helen, and Pauline were the only ones who didn't pass the examination.

7a. As we expected, Bill didn't arrive on time.
 b. Bill didn't arrive on time as we'd expected.

8a. She listened for a moment. The radio upstairs was playing a curious piece of jazz.
 b. The radio upstairs was playing a curious piece of jazz. She listened for a moment.

9a. We're very proud of this painting of our son's.
 b. We're very proud of this painting of our son.

10a. I went to the chemists and explained what I wanted.
 b. I went to the chemist's and explained what I wanted.

11a. She has accepted the job which will let her live in London.
 b. She has accepted the job, which will let her live in London.

12a. They went out of their way to see Richard home.
 b. They went out of their way to see Richard's home.

13a. Philip said John was a silly idiot.
 b. Philip, said John, was a silly idiot.

14a. We decided to stop for the night at the first hotel which had a private bathroom.
  b. We decided to stop for the night at the first hotel, which had a private bathroom.

15a. He wondered how I could ever get together enough money for the project.
  b. He wondered: 'How could I ever get together enough money for the project?'

16a. He arrived in time. The ceremony had not begun.
  b. He arrived on time. The ceremony had not begun.

17a. She tried to push the car to start it, but without success.
  b. She tried pushing the car to start it, but without success.

18a. Peter dared to ask me for a rise, in spite of the lack of business.
  b. Peter dared me to ask for a rise, in spite of the lack of business.

19a. Don't rush away. I have to tell you something that will interest you.
  b. Don't rush away. I have something to tell you that will interest you.

20a. She stopped to look at the jeweller's window.
  b. She stopped looking at the jeweller's window.

21a. I remember telling my pupils that there would not be any lessons the next day.
  b. I remembered to tell my pupils that there would not be any lessons the next day.

22a. You must try not to do that again.
  b. You must not try to do that again.

23a. At the beginning, we imagined that it might be very difficult to do it.
  b. We imagined that it might be very difficult to do it at the beginning.

24a. You can be pleased about little that you have done for us.
  b. You can be pleased about the little that you have done for us.

25a. He would like to have met her.
  b. He would have liked to meet her.

Eight

Put the italicised words in these 20 sentences at the beginning of each sentence. Make any alterations to these words or to the rest of the sentences that are necessary to produce grammatically correct results.

Example: 'A body fell *out of the wardrobe*!'
Answer: '*Out of the wardrobe* fell a body!'

1. Marilyn sleeps *so soundly* that she wouldn't be woken by even a jazz-band playing in her room.
2. The rain came *down* in buckets.
3. He fell *down* the stairs.
4. I shall *never* set foot in their house again.
5. I shall never set foot in their house again *in any circumstances*. (*Careful!*)
6. The cat jumped *up* on to her lap.
7. We have *hardly ever* seen her smile.
8. You must not *on any* account take more than two of these pills at a time.
9. If anybody *should* find my wallet and return it to me, I'd be the most grateful man alive.
10. He *not* only complained about the food, he also tore up the bill and threw it on the floor.
11. I have *seldom* seen such a beautiful girl.
12. They went all the way *in vain*. The shop was shut.
13. The poor maid fell *into a flower-bed* when she was cleaning the windows.
14. I have never seen anything like this *anywhere* in the world.
15. A good result can be achieved *only* like this.
16. You said that *with very good reason*.
17. He went *to such lengths* with his lateness every morning that he simply had to be given the sack.
18. I tripped *over*, to my great annoyance.
19. Paul tripped *over*, to his great annoyance.
20. Timothy's pomposity is *so* annoying that one wants to kick him round the square.

Nine

After-life

Here are 25 'head-words' which are printed in capital letters. Below each 'head-word' there are six other words. Some, but not all, of these can combine with the 'head-word' to form an accepted compound, *with the 'head-word' coming first in the compound.* In some cases the compound needs a hyphen; in other cases it does not.

Say a. which words can combine with the 'head-words' to form an accepted compound;
b. what the compound means;
c. whether a hyphen is needed or not.

Example: ROAD
side
speed
house
path
police
way

Answer: There are three accepted compounds:
i. *Roadside;* i.e. the strip of free ground which commonly borders a road on either side. No hyphen is needed.
ii. *Road-house;* i.e. a large restaurant or hotel situated in the country on one of the main roads. A hyphen is needed.
iii. *Roadway;* i.e. the highway; that part of a road used by vehicles. No hyphen.

1. POST	2. TEST	3. WHIP	4. OIL
script	table	round	cloth
letter	case	well	pan
card	tube	lash	can
room	man	cord	field
mark	room	hand	coat
date	place	box	skins

5. SUNDAY	6. SAND	7. WORK	8. MONEY
bread	paper	house	lender
best	boy	shop	making
cloth	stone	flat	sacks
school	floor	room	bags
time	fly	full	smell
ride	wasp	shy	box

9. MOUTH	10. AFTER	11. SAFETY	12. OUT
shape	thought	place	cast
piece	think	razor	throw
teeth	feeling	room	see
organ	nuisance	match	look
place	joy	pin	wit
moisture	life	needle	size

13. RUN	14. UNDER	15. WINDOW	16. SUN
away	cat	view	stroke
way	dog	pane	chair
route	man	piece	heat
ground	wear	sill	burn
about	hand	shine	beam
girl	leg	man	down

17. OVER	18. RED	19. FLOOR	20. UP
ocean	handed	carpet	lift
seas	hot	rug	right
sky	telegram	show	left
dose	herring	walker	roar
rule	letter	bell	start
go	fish	cloth	stop

21. TOOTH	22. IN	23. BLOOD	24. LIGHT
ache	go	warmth	house
pain	come	heat	weight
doctor	born	group	year
brush	joy	hound	month
pick	doors	quarrel	fingered
soap	look	feud	faced

25. DOOR

keeper	way	pin
holder	mat	nail

Ten

Change these 20 sentences into their passive forms.
Some will require only the simple, basic change:

Example: 'They are preparing the meal.'
Answer: 'The meal is being prepared.'

But others will require the more complicated change which uses an infinitive:

Example: 'They say that it was a good party.'
Answer: 'It's said *to have been* a good party.'

1. Somebody has burnt a hole in this carpet.
2. They are building a new aerodrome there.
3. Rumour says that the Princess is expecting a baby.
4. Some people think that this portrait, which has no signature, was painted by Da Vinci.
5. The students have said that Susan Kerr is the most beautiful girl in the college this term.

6. It disappoints me that the Council has adopted that policy.
7. People expect that the Home Secretary will resign.
8. They will be overhauling the machines all day tomorrow.
9. They are going to do it while we watch.
10. They have built an extremely good new road between Belgrade and the Greek frontier.
11. Most people believed that he had been telling the truth.
12. The radio reports that all out-going flights have been cancelled because of the fog.
13. They have offered him the Presidency.
14. The radio reports that the Cabinet has resigned.
15. The newspaper says that our Professor is being considered for that top job.
16. Everybody knows that this machine is by far the best.
17. He has had to do it all over again.
18. Someone had let the air out of the tyres and they couldn't move the car. They had to borrow a bicycle from a cottage nearby and fetch a car from the village.
19. Last night's paper said that poor Mary Moppet has had her throat cut.
20. People assume only too easily that politics solve all human problems. No one ought ever to make so false an assumption.

Eleven

In these 25 sentences, the verbs in brackets are given in one basic infinitive form, which may or may not be correct in the sentence. If this form is not correct, some other form must take its place. If, for example, you have the infinitive (*give*) you may replace it by *to give*, *gives*, *gave*, *giving*, *given*—or you may leave it as it is in the brackets.

Say which form is appropriate for the meaning of each sentence. (In some cases you may find that two different forms are equally correct.)

Example: 'You ought (have) (be) (listen) all the time.'
Answer: 'You ought *to have been listening* all the time.'

1. Philip loves (give) outdoor barbecue parties.
2. You are not yet used to (take) orders, I (see).
3. We (have) (be) (look) for a house like this since we got married.
4. I wish I (speak) as many languages as you (do).
5. She used (play) tennis very well indeed.
6. You seem (have) (be) (make) a lot of progress since I (see) you last.
7. Beethoven's Fifth (be) (go) (be) (play) at eight on the radio tonight.
8. I ought not (have) (forget) his birthday.
9. We shall probably (have) (pay) a fine for leaving the car here so long.
10. He (be) (plan) (go) to America soon.

11. Why do you always put off that job? You (have) (be) (go) (do) it every day this month, but you don't keep your word.
12. Last night I (think) it (be) (go) (snow).
13. If we can (afford) it next year, we'll (have) the front of the house (paint) again.
14. I (have) (grow) accustomed to not (believe) what he tells me.
15. The children ought (be) (get) ready for bed now.
16. That type of skirt (be) now (be) (wear) again.
17. Peter is behaving more correctly today, isn't he? He must (have) (be) (speak) to!
18. You must be wrong. He can't (have) (forget) that he was (invite). He (be) probably on the way.
19. I wish we could stop him (make) such a fool of himself.
20. They decided (ask) him (resign).
21. My hair needs (cut) badly.
22. I'd prefer anybody but her (dance) with.
23. Would you mind (come) back again tomorrow at about the same time?
24. He would (have) (explain) it again for you if he (have) (know) that you (have) not (understand).
25. We should (have) (like) (be) there with you.

Twelve

This is a test of your ability to *assimilate* the full meaning of something that you read.

What to do:
1. Read each piece once—ONLY ONCE.
2. Cover the piece with a slip of paper or something similar, and read the sentences *a*, *b*, *c*, *d* below it.[1] Only *one* of these is correct.
3. Decide which of these four sentences is the correct one. *Do not cheat by looking back at the piece again! Make your decision first.*

   Example: Dr Drew has a younger brother and a couple of sisters, both older than he is. Including Dr Drew and his parents, how many members are there in his immediate family?
                                          a. Three?
                                          b. Six?
                                          c. Four?
                                          d. Five?

   Answer: b.

---

[1] If you can get somebody to read everything to you, *so that you test your ear too*, the exercise will be even more valuable.

1. No matter how hard I try to understand my brother's point of view, I nearly always find myself in violent disagreement with his beliefs and principles.

> *Read this once, and then cover it!*
> *Make your decision without reading it again.*

   a. I am beginning to dislike my brother.
   b. He has some violent beliefs and principles.
   c. I see things in a different way.
   d. He is wrong most of the time.

2. When my father-in-law goes from London to Brighton every second weekend, he prefers to go by train instead of by car. Although he doesn't always manage to find a seat, he finds the train journey less tiring. There is much too much traffic on the London-Brighton road these days, he says.

   a. My father-in-law goes to Brighton twice a month.
   b. He doesn't go by train because he can never find a seat.
   c. He goes by train because he always finds a seat.
   d. He doesn't need his car in Brighton.

3. Bill said that in his youth he had often lived outside his own country. He had lived in Spain, in Greece, in Persia, and in the United States. However interesting these countries were, however lavish the hospitality of their inhabitants, he had never been free from the ache of homesickness.

   a. Bill felt homesick for Spain, Greece, Persia and the United States.
   b. He had longed to be in his own country.
   c. Hospitality in those other countries was greater than in his own.
   d. His own country was not very interesting to him in his youth.

4. When they are away during the summer at the Boy Scouts' Camp, the boys make their own beds, wash the dishes, and even sometimes cook their own food. They go out exploring the countryside, prospecting for minerals, studying wild-life, picking berries, collecting birds'-eggs, and so on.

   a. The boys sometimes cook birds'-eggs.
   b. They prospect for berries.
   c. In the camp there is a lot of wild-life.
   d. They are learning how to look after themselves.

5. For some years, a research unit in America has been carrying out a scientific study into the causes of road accidents. These investigations have uncovered some surprising and significant facts.

   a. A scientific study is now being made into an accident that happened to a research unit in America some years ago.

15

b. There have been, for some years, a surprising and significant number of accidents in America.

c. A research unit in America has been surprised by some of the facts its investigations have uncovered.

d. One significant fact about road accidents in America is that a research unit is now making a scientific study of their causes.

6. The ancient Greeks speculated about the origin, history and structure of language. The Romans then constructed Latin grammars on the Greek model. But it is only within the last century or so that languages have been studied in a scientific way by careful, comprehensive research and observation.

a. The study of grammar is relatively new.
b. The Greeks wrote the most useful grammars.
c. The study of languages is now based on scientific approaches.
d. The Romans taught Latin to the Greeks.

7. When the middle-aged professor reached the top of the long, steep hill, he got off his bicycle and sat down for a while in the shade of a tree. Why do you suppose he stopped?

a. Because the next stretch was downhill?
b. Because the climb had been tiring?
c. Because the next climb was going to be more tiring and he wanted to get back his strength?
d. Because he wanted to while away the time in the shade of a tree?

8. Although the students arrived at the institute only the day before yesterday, which was Monday, they showed in today's entrance examinations that they are qualified to begin their lessons on the first day of next term—the day after tomorrow. When will that be?

a. Friday?
b. Wednesday?
c. Saturday?
d. Thursday?

9. It was amazing to see, as the war went on, how the Army accumulated 'experts'. They started to build up immediately after Dunkirk and went on until, by the end, we had experts on very nearly anything you could think of, and on one or two things that you probably wouldn't have dreamed of.

a. The Army was amazed to see its experts at Dunkirk.
b. Army experts were unknown before Dunkirk.
c. After Dunkirk the Army wouldn't have dreamed of accumulating experts.
d. After Dunkirk the number of experts in the Army began to grow.

16

10. A poor man entered a doctor's consulting-room. He looked very unhappy. 'Doctor,' he said, 'you must help me. I swallowed a penny about a month ago.' 'Good heavens, man!' said the doctor. 'Why have you waited so long? Why didn't you come to me on the day that you swallowed it?' 'To tell you the truth, Doctor,' the poor man replied, 'I didn't need the money so badly then.'

a. The poor man's financial position was better some time ago.
b. The poor man swallowed a penny in the doctor's consulting-room.
c. The doctor charged only a penny because his visitor was such a poor man.
d. The doctor said he should not have waited a whole month before coming for help.

Thirteen
contemptible   contemptuous

Here are 25 pairs of words that are often confused. Make sentences to show that you understand the difference in their meanings.

1. judicial
   judicious
	7. continual
	   continuous
		13. effective
		    efficient

2. prudent
   prudish
	8. contemptible
	   contemptuous
		14. licence
		    license

3. economic
   economical
	9. goal
	   gaol
		15. ingenuous
		    ingenious

4. historic
   historical
	10. emigrate
	    immigrate
		16. imperial
		    imperious

5. childish
   childlike
	11. illegible
	    eligible
		17. incredulous
		    incredible

6. epigram
   epitaph
	12. effect
	    affect
		18. human
		    humane

19. imminent	22. story	25. punctual
eminent	storey	punctilious
20. esteem	23. sensible	
estimate	sensitive	
21. genus	24. popular	
genius	populous	

Fourteen

If we say 'Come on. Let's *put our heads together*.', we mean that we must consider or discuss some problem together. And if we tell a child that '*he must keep a stiff upper lip*', we are advising him, through an idiomatic expression, to keep up his courage in situations that might make him want to cry.

A. Here are a dozen other idiomatic expressions. Can you say what they mean?
1. I've got his name *on the tip of my tongue*.
2. We'd better *lie low* for a week or so.
3. She made him *eat humble pie* before forgiving him.
4. I went to him *hat in hand*, but he wouldn't help.
5. The whole thing was only *a storm in a tea-cup*.
6. *Go and tell that to the Marines!*
7. Yes, there's no doubt that *she wears the trousers*.
8. Has he, perhaps, got *his tongue in his cheek*?
9. You'll *get into hot water*, I'm afraid, for this.
10. Why have you got such *a long face* today?
11. *Before you could say Jack Robinson*, he disappeared.
12. I think you'd better go and *pour some oil on those troubled waters*.

B. At a time during the Second World War when things were going very badly for England, a well-known beer manufacturer issued the following advertisement. It did us good because it made us laugh— and it made us laugh because it played with a number of commonly-used idiomatic expressions.

Can you explain them? And can you say why the various things were 'demanded by the situation' at that time?[1]

---

[1]Suppose, for example, one of the items were 'STIFF UPPER LIP for keeping', it would mean that everybody had *to keep a stiff upper lip* (i.e. to keep up his courage) in those difficult and often tragic times.

WHAT THE SITUATION DEMANDS

1. WHEEL *for putting shoulder to*

2. SOCKS *for pulling up*

3. STONE *for not leaving unturned*

4. BRASS TACKS *for getting down to*

5. TRUMP CARD *for playing*

6. BOLD FACE *for putting on it*

7. BELT *for tightening*

8. GUINNESS *for strength* [1]

[1] This is the advertisement for the beer.

Fifteen

Put the following into Reported (Indirect) Speech. (*Be careful not to use the verb 'to say' more often in the reported version than is absolutely necessary.*)

Example: 'Would you bring me my mackintosh when you come downstairs,' said Patricia to John. 'It's begun to rain quite heavily.'

Answer: Patricia asked John to bring her her mackintosh when he came downstairs. It had begun to rain quite heavily.

1. 'The trouble with you,' James said to his brother, 'is that you don't want to understand anything outside your own business.'
2. 'There is now no danger at all,' said the policewoman. 'You can all leave whenever you like.'
3. 'Have you any idea where Peter has gone?' Mr Togg said to his wife. 'He's awfully late. I'm getting worried about him.'
4. 'At last,' said my father, 'I can feel sure that they have really done their best.'
5. 'My mackintosh is getting shabby,' Patricia said to John. 'Will you buy me a new one, darling?'
6. 'Will you buy me a new mackintosh, darling?' Patricia said to John. 'Mine is getting shabby.'
7. 'If ever I were to win a big prize in the National Lottery,' Maureen said yesterday, 'I shouldn't buy a car or a mink or a diamond ring, I should buy a little house beside the sea.'
8. The pretty air-hostess stopped me as I was getting up out of my seat, and said: 'We're going to take off in a moment or so, sir. Would you please sit down again and fasten your seat belt.' She looked at my cigarette and smiled. 'I'm afraid that you will have to stop smoking too, sir—at least for the next little while.'
9. Lady Harlow chuckled and said: 'Alan pretends, in front of me, that he doesn't drink. Personally, I like a glass of sherry now and again. Will you please give me one? Give yourself one, too.'
10. 'Yes, she's an odd girl, is Leah,' said Tim, looking me full in the eyes. 'I feel very sorry for her. You do realise she's in love with you, I suppose? Even *you* couldn't fail to have seen *that*!'
11. 'Among people who claim to be gentlemen,' said Pat contemptuously, 'one has to assume that the truth is being told—until the lie is revealed. Go away, Smith, and think that over for a little while.'
12. Mrs Sanders (on the telephone): 'This is Mary Sanders. I have an appointment with Dr Bodger at six o'clock tomorrow. I'm awfully sorry but I simply have to cancel it. My brother is arriving unexpectedly from the Argentine at about three o'clock and the whole family is going to the airport to meet him. But please tell Dr Bodger how sorry I am.'

13. My guest said, as I asked him to sit down, 'But which is your own chair? I'm sure you must have your own special one.'
14. 'OUCH!' yelled Richard, as he hit his thumb with the hammer. 'Hell! Damn! Blast!'
15. He said to me: 'Please be as quiet as you can.'
16. She said to me: 'I think you're a better doctor than your partner, so I'll do what *you* advise.'
17. When he arrived home, he looked very ill. 'Go to bed at once,' ordered his wife. 'You look like death warmed up! Whatever's wrong with you?'
18. 'They weren't at home,' said Susan. 'I rang and rang, but there was no sign of life in the house.'
19. 'Have you seen the children's room?' said my wife hysterically. 'Have I produced a race of barbarians? Everything breakable has been broken. There might have been some sort of civil war there!'
20. Frank ran up to the policeman. 'My car's been stolen,' he gasped.
21. 'It was most unwise,' the Headmaster said to me, 'to rag the new History Master like that. You'll have to be punished quite severely. Bring me, please, the cane that you will find in the cupboard that is just behind you.'
22. 'Rubbish!' the worker said to the foreman. 'Nonsense! Bosh!'
23. 'Mmmmm!' said Billy, as the waitress put the ice-cream in front of him.
24. 'Do not lean out of the window,' said the notice in the railway carriage.
25. 'I wish we had brought some lighter clothes with us,' said Susan. 'This part of the world gets hotter in summer than I realised.'

Sixteen

There are a good many colloquial comparisons in English like
as good as gold,
as brown as a berry,
which mean, simply, *extremely* good (as far as behaviour is concerned) and *extremely* brown (as far as sun-tan is concerned).

Here are 20 incomplete comparisons. Can you complete them? Can you say what they concern?

1. as ...... as the hills.
2. as ...... as honey.
3. as ...... as a feather.
4. as ...... as a sandboy.
5. as ...... as a mule.
6. as ...... as dust.
7. as ...... as a poker.
8. as ...... as a flash.
9. as ...... as a daisy.
10. as ...... as the driven snow.
11. as poor as a ....
12. as black as ....
13. as sound as a ....
14. as mad as a ....

15. as cold as ....
16. as firm as a ....
17. as bright as a ....
18. as deaf as a ....
19. as mischievous as a ....
20. as easy as ....

Seventeen

. . . introduced to him once upon a time

Here are 25 sentences, each of which has one grammatical mistake. Can you say what is the mistake, and why it is a mistake?

1. Oh yes, they are married a very long time now.
2. The stones on that beach are sharp. One ought to wear shoes. Otherwise one may cut his feet badly.
3. However hard I try, I can never succeed to arrive before the boss.
4. We have been introduced to him once upon a time.
5. He has no one of the charm of his father.
6. I don't go to the cinema very often nowadays because I use to study three or four hours every night for the examination next month.
7. I don't know how to begin to thank you. You are really the most generous.
8. In life, a humour is as necessary as health.
9. That clock, that we had repaired only last week, has stopped again.
10. The doctor said to him to go to bed and stay there.
11. The news are a good deal better this morning.
12. That is the Duke's of Brentwood castle.
13. He told that he might be a bit late today.
14. This is one of the best films that has ever been made.
15. He is an officer of great courage and who has received many decorations.
16. He deserves his riches because he has worked very hardly all his life.
17. A wet Sunday can be put to good use by doing all the things that we have been putting off doing.
18. There's a very good, opened last year motel quite near the frontier, if you want to break your journey.
19. No, we shall not go there unless we shall be asked.

20. You know, between you and I, I think he may not be telling the truth.
21. No, sir! I deny it absolutely. I have never and I could never do such a thing.
22. Nobody liked the meal but I. I thought it very tasty indeed.
23. Being such a miserable morning, I decided to stay in bed.
24. He went neither to the cinema or to the theatre during the whole of last term.
25. This curry tastes hot, just like it should.

Eighteen

A. Rewrite this telegram in the form of a letter:

GRATEFUL YOUR INVITATION PARTICIPATE GLASSMAKERS CONFERENCE STOP IMPOSSIBLE ARRIVE PROPOSED DATE BUT COULD COME SEVENTEENTH REMAINING TILL END STOP PRESUME ALL EXPENSES PAID YOUR ASSOCIATION PLUS REASONABLE FEE STOP PLEASE CABLE AGREEMENT NEW DATE AND STATE TERMS STOP INFORM IF ACCOMMODATION AVAILABLE WIFE STOP LANT

B. Here are some cryptic newspaper headlines. See if you can guess what they were supposed to mean.

1. PRIME MINISTER MOVES TO CUT DOWN EXPENDITURE
2. NEWFIELD WIFE TO BE STRANGLED
3. WOMEN MAN WINNING YACHT
4. DOG IN WELL DRAMA: NEW RESCUE ATTEMPT TODAY
5. MODEL MURDER: JUDGE WITHDRAWS
6. GOVERNMENT REBELS REFUSE WHIP
7. £1½M. LOSS WIPED OUT
8. SMOKING BILL THROWN OUT BY LORDS
9. HOME SECRETARY UNDER FIRE AGAIN
10. EGG TALKS: AGRICULTURAL ADVISERS MEET

Nineteen

The word *previous* does not rhyme with the word *precious* although both have all the same letters save one. Similarly, *proved* does not rhyme with *shoved*, although the last four letters of each word are the same.[1]
In these 25 pairs, the endings of the words are the same, but they do not rhyme. Can you say how they are all pronounced?

---

[1] The pronunciations of the four words are:
    priːvjəs   `prefəs   pruːvd   ʃʌvd

1. horse—worse
2. eight—height
3. beard—heard
4. sounded—wounded
5. slaughter—laughter
6. desirable—admirable
7. forward—reward
8. cigar—scholar
9. exile—simile
10. borough—hiccough
11. pork—work
12. south—youth
13. cost—post
14. pleat—sweat
15. monkey—donkey
16. finger—singer
17. worry—sorry
18. rather—bather
19. break—creak
20. fury—bury
21. father—lather
22. wolf—golf
23. examining—combining
24. wallet—mallet
25. banquet—parquet

Twenty

When a noun in English ends with the letter 'o', its plural is formed sometimes with the addition of the letters 'es', sometimes with the addition of the letter 's' only, and sometimes in both ways.

A. Say how the plurals of these 20 nouns are made.

B. Give a concise definition (as though for a dictionary) of as many of their meanings as you know.

1. tomato
2. potato
3. piano
4. casino
5. ghetto
6. motto
7. echo
8. hero
9. manifesto
10. soprano
11. oratorio
12. studio
13. mosquito
14. crescendo
15. volcano
16. proviso
17. stiletto
18. peccadillo
19. memento
20. innuendo

Twenty-one

. . . horse in the mouth

Here are 25 English proverbs with one word missing from each. Below each proverb three words are printed. Can you say which word belongs to the proverb? And then can you say what the proverb means?

Example: A fool and his _____ are soon parted.
   money   *friends*   *wife*

Answer: money.
   A foolish person quickly and wastefully spends all his money.

1. Don't look a _____ horse in the mouth.
   wild   *sick*   *gift*

2. A bird in the hand is worth two in the _____.
   cage   *bush*   *stomach*

3. As you make your _____, so you must lie on it.
   bed   *carpet*   *cushion*

4. Birds of a _____ flock together.
   family   *feather*   *species*

5. _____ is thicker than water.
   Whisky   *Blood*   *Soup*

6. You can't get blood out of a _____.
   chicken   *stone*   *mother-in-law*

7. Those who live in _____ houses shouldn't throw stones.
   country   *glass*   *paper*

8. All is not _____ that glitters.
   anger   *jealousy*   *gold*

9. When Greek meets _____, then comes the tug of war!
   Greek   *politicians*   *flatterers*

10. Make _____ while the sun shines.
    friends   whoopee   hay

11. Where ignorance is bliss, 'tis folly to be _____.
    ambitious   wise   educated

12. It's an _____ wind that blows nobody any good.
    ill   angry   east

13. In for a penny, in for a _____.
    hundred   pound   halfpenny

14. The labourer is worthy of his _____.
    hire   rest   work

15. What is _____ for the goose is sauce for the gander.
    mustard   tasty   sauce

16. Every _____ has a silver lining.
    jewel-box   cloud   quarrel

17. A miss is as good as a _____.
    mile   madam   mother

18. A fault confessed is _____ redressed.
    already   half   always

19. Never say _____.
    damn!   never   die

20. A rolling stone _____ no moss.
    gathers   flattens   grows

21. A stitch in time saves _____.
    time   nine   twenty

22. One man's _____ is another man's poison.
    drink   medicine   meat

23. It never rains but it _____.
    snows   pours   drizzles

24. Let not the sun go down upon thy _____.
    hopes   wrath   windows

25. He who _____ the piper calls the tune.
    pays   marries   invites

Twenty-two

Decide whether the blank spaces below need 'a' ('an'), 'the', or no article at all.

Example: 'Ouzo is _____ aperitif that contains _____ anise. Until anything is added to it, it has _____ appearance of _____ water. When anything is added, it begins to look like _____ milk.'

Answer: 'Ouzo is *an* aperitif that contains anise. Until anything is added to it, it has *the* appearance of water. When anything is added, it begins to look like milk.'

1. The kitten crouched outside _____ gates of _____ American Embassy in _____ Belgrade. It uttered _____ frightened cry every three seconds and gave _____ hiss whenever anyone passed.

Lilian, cutting _____ roses in _____ garden, went to _____ gates as soon as she heard _____ cries. 'You poor little thing,' she said, and picked _____ animal up. She had _____ weakness for _____ stray cats. This was _____ cause of _____ continual friction with her parents, for they, though fond of _____ cats in _____ normal way, did not share her enthusiasm for collecting them.

With _____ kitten spitting and struggling in her arms, Lilian walked across _____ lawn into _____ house. She put out _____ arm to close _____ front door behind her. _____ kitten seized its chance, wrenched itself free, leapt to _____ ground, bolted across _____ hall and up _____ wide staircase. It vanished into _____ room on _____ first landing.

2. _____ light drizzle fell over _____ city of _____ Salzburg. _____ lights of _____ shops twinkled in _____ gathering dusk. _____ church clock struck _____ hour of _____ six.

The young man walked slowly along _____ glistening pavement. He came to _____ momentary stop in _____ front of each shop-window and studied its contents with _____ wholly false interest.

The two plain-clothes policemen, _____ hundred yards behind him, sauntered along _____ street without making any pretence at studying _____ shop-windows. There was no need for _____ pretence, because _____ young man knew that he was being followed. When he stopped at _____ shop-window, they simply came to _____ relaxed halt until he moved on to _____ next one.

_____ young man stopped _____ little longer at _____ bookshop. _____ policemen came to _____ halt again. _____ one of them took _____ packet of _____ cigarettes from _____ pocket and offered it to _____ other. _____ young man watched them out of _____ corner of his eye. He saw their heads bend as they lit _____ cigarettes in _____ rain. He turned and walked quickly into _____ Zipfer Bar _____ few yards away.

3. Peter Merrill stood at __1__ one of __2__ windows of __3__ Rome Airport and watched __4__ rapid approach of __5__ Comet that was carrying his wife. It came down with __6__ great grace but at what seemed to him __7__ alarming speed. He drew __8__ breath and held it.

__9__ Comet was, in fact, travelling at 140 miles __10__ hour as it touched __11__ ground at __12__ beginning of __13__ two-mile-long runway. It was silent until its jets were put into __14__ reverse, as __15__ brake, and then __16__ deafening noise made him jump. When he saw that __17__ great machine was safely down on __18__ ground he let out __19__ breath he had taken, and went back to __20__ bar to wait for __21__ passengers to be cleared by __22__ customs and __23__ immigration police.

4. __1__ sun was beginning to set on __2__ evening in __3__ late autumn, several thousand years ago. Two travellers walked tiredly to __4__ edge of __5__ stream they had seen and sat down under __6__ tree. They took off __7__ dusty sandals they were wearing and put their tired feet into __8__ cold water.

__9__ older man leaned back on __10__ elbow, turned his head, and looked at __11__ valley along which they had been walking all __12__ day. He was __13__ very big, strong man, with __14__ fine head and __15__ iron-grey beard. He watched __16__ lights appearing, __17__ one after __18__ other, in __19__ far-away houses and cottages of __20__ valley.

5. __1__ outbreak of __2__ fire at __3__ base of __4__ oil-well is usually extinguished by __5__ explosion of __6__ nitroglycerine. __7__ long tubular container, filled with __8__ explosive, is dropped down __9__ shaft of __10__ well. When it hits __11__ ground at __12__ bottom of __13__ shaft, it explodes and momentarily removes __14__ oxygen from __15__ air there. Since __16__ fire cannot exist without __17__ oxygen, __18__ flames at __19__ base of __20__ well are extinguished instantaneously.

Twenty-three

Say where the strong stress lies in these 40 words.

Example: recognise
Answer: re*cognise*

1. contribution
2. necessary
3. parental
4. contributory
5. necessity
6. ceremony
7. parallel
8. mackintosh

28

9. advertiser
10. ceremonial
11. execute
12. circumstances
13. catholic
14. collapse
15. accumulate
16. uppermost
17. advertisement
18. cement
19. catholicism
20. massacre
21. benevolent
22. horizon
23. appreciate
24. interesting

25. character
26. refuse (*noun*)
27. minute (*adjective*)
28. monopoly
29. operation
30. radiator
31. anxiety
32. emphasis
33. informative
34. operative
35. architect
36. mature
37. nature
38. architectural
39. radiation
40. mechanical

Twenty-four

In simple language, and without using technical terms, explain how to do these things:

1. make an omelette.
2. shave, with an electric razor.
3. sew a button on to a shirt or dress.
4. shave, with soap and an ordinary razor.
5. make a bed.
6. change the wheel of a car.
7. thread a needle.
8. load and fire a rifle or shotgun.
9. repair a laddered stocking.
10. repair a leaking tap.
11. press a woollen skirt.
12. grill a chicken over a camp-fire.
13. paint your finger-nails.
14. lay and light a coal-fire.
15. wash and dry your hair.
16. plant a small tree in the garden.
17. remove a splinter from someone's hand.
18. send a telegram over the telephone.
19. clean and dress a badly-lacerated knee.
20. take a good indoor photograph.

Twenty-five

. . . as though she had seen a ghost

Put the following into Direct Speech.

Example: Harold suggested that they should all go to Brighton for the week-end. It would do them good to have a change. He asked David whether he would like to join them.

Answer: 'Let's all go to Brighton for the week-end,' said Harold. 'It will do us good to have a change. Would you like to join us, David?'

1. Helen asked me to buy her a diamond ring which a friend of hers was offering very cheaply.
2. They said they had learned the proper way to make tea when they were in England in 1964.
3. I told him to be more thoughtful. It was very unkind to make so much noise outside a sick person's bedroom window.
4. He explained that he was late once again at the office because there was a strike, as I knew, of the trolley-bus workers. He hadn't been able to get on an ordinary bus. They were all so full that they didn't stop for anyone. He hoped I would excuse him.
5. Patricia asked me if I knew the Bells at all well.
6. Madeleine exclaimed at the beauty of the sunset.
7. Jonathan asked me to lend him £100.
8. He told us that the only reason that he was selling his car was that he was being sent abroad and he couldn't take it with him. He asked us to let him know as quickly as possible if we decided to buy it.
9. Bowing gallantly, Roderick asked Pauline if he might have the pleasure of a dance.
10. The fat man told Leila that she mustn't take him too seriously.
11. John swore as he cut himself while shaving.
12. The waitress put a dish in front of me, apologised for the time it had taken, and hoped it was what I had ordered.

30

13. Bernard explained that their cocktail-party had had to be cancelled because Maria had developed an inflammation of her appendix. She might have to have an operation.
14. Richard told us he would have phoned us if it had been possible. There was simply not a telephone to be found, though.
15. The policeman on the motor-cycle overtook the car and waved it to the side of the road. He then asked the driver if he knew what speed he had been doing.
16. I told the maid to wake me at seven-thirty the following morning.
17. He said it was a bit chilly. He was going to put a pullover on. I ought to do the same.
18. Mother said she was tired. She suggested that we should all stop working for half an hour. We needed a breathing space.
19. Eleanor murmured in admiration as Roger walked through the door, resplendent in full-dress uniform, decorations and orders.
20. Mark asked Mrs Johnson if he might bring her dog a bone from time to time.
21. The captain said he thought they would be inside the harbour before sundown.
22. Bill asked Mary whether anything was wrong. She looked as though she had seen a ghost.
23. They asked the doctor to come as quickly as ever he could. The old lady was sinking rapidly.
24. Mrs Monroe told her husband that there was no sense in his getting worn out fighting a bat. They are terribly quick. And, in any case, she added, it would hang by its feet pretty soon and go to sleep. It wouldn't hurt him. He needn't be afraid.
25. Mr Monroe retorted irritably that he was terribly quick too. And he was *not* afraid that the bat would hurt him. He simply wanted to find something to kill it with. He couldn't find anything in his room. That was the only reason why he had run into hers.

Twenty-six

In each of these 20 standard expressions, the blank space can be filled with only one of the four words which are printed in italics beneath it. Choose this word.

Example: 'I'm tired. Let's have a ...... space.'
      rest   *breathing*   *clear*   *blank*
Answer: 'Let's have a *breathing* space.'

1. When his father spoke to him, it acted like ....
   a marvel   *wonder*   *magic*   *joy*

2. His house was a ...... between a palace and a hotel.
   combination   *union*   *cross*   *link*

3. Sometimes we have to be ...... to be kind.
   mean   *callous*   *crude*   *cruel*

4. I'm tired of talking about money. Let's change the ....
   argument   *tune*   *record*   *subject*

5. It's time he got to ...... with his problems.
   brass tacks   *reason*   *grips*   *wrestle*

6. Everybody talked about it. It was a nine days' ....
   glory   *marvel*   *surprise*   *wonder*

7. She wouldn't hurt him for ....
   worlds   *heaven's sake*   *everything*   *the moon*

8. Since his wife died, he's gone to ....
   pieces   *fragments*   *bits*   *scraps*

9. It was his ambition to meet Maria Callas in the ....
   street   *face*   *flesh*   *skin*

10. No one in his ...... would have done such a thing.
    intelligence   *reason*   *senses*   *mind*

11. His name is on the ...... of my tongue.
    edge   *tip*   *point*   *top*

12. From now on everything will be ...... sailing.
    simple   *straight*   *plain*   *pretty*

13. After working so hard all day I slept like a ....
    log   *dormouse*   *mole*   *dog*

14. I think you're pulling my ....
    limb   *nose*   *coat*   *leg*

15. He was an artist to his finger ....
    ends   *nails*   *tips*   *prints*

16. I've got a bone to ...... with you.
    pick   *share*   *part*   *divide*

17. He hasn't got the courage of his ....
    convictions   *knowledge*   *name*   *fears*

18. They'll give you a good run for your ....
    horse   *rope*   *hare*   *money*

19. It's a great pity, but he has let himself go to ...... recently. He must pull himself together.
    ruin   *seed*   *shabbiness*   *old-age*

20. Are you trying to pull the ...... over my eyes?
    cover   *wool*   *cotton*   *glasses*

Twenty-seven

Look at these six words:

cow   so   zoo   shoe   star   chair

They each contain a different consonant sound (represented by the letters underlined). Write each one at the head of a separate list. Then arrange the following 50 words below them so that all those containing the same consonant sounds (underlined) are in the same list. (Note that the lists will not all contain the same number of words.)

1. crease	14. eggs	27. precise	40. science
2. chaos	15. whips	28. charade	41. cholera
3. phase	16. western	29. condition	42. fission
4. maze	17. fasten	30. cushion	43. refusal
5. sure	18. charm	31. ration	44. hasten
6. despise	19. chemist	32. schedule	45. chorus
7. easy	20. cease	33. scheme	46. chore
8. pistol	21. whistle	34. phrase	47. chime
9. chase	22. ache	35. case	48. rustle
10. scissors	23. tease	36. gas	49. siphon
11. possession	24. sugar	37. cause	50. cipher
12. parachute	25. mustard	38. choir	
13. glisten	26. erase	39. raise	

Twenty-eight

Complete each of these 20 sentences by adding the words or groups of words that are shown below in italics in the order which seems to you to be the most natural. (Do not split up the groups themselves.)

Example: 'They live in a ....'
cottage   little   by the sea   pretty
Answer: 'They live in a pretty little cottage by the sea.'

1. They have lived ....
before the war   just   there   since

2. In January, ...
bought   beautiful   ikons   old   from that shop   three   I

3. She was carrying ....
rubberised-silk   over her free arm   white   a   mackintosh   flimsy

4. He lived in ....
very   to be built   the   pre-fabricated   first   in 1943   houses   of   one

5. My friend's house was ....
   most   obtainable   full   oriental   the   of   in London
   expensive   carpets

6. Between here and there ....
   there   straight   beautiful   motorway   ruler   a   a   is
   is   as   as   now   almost   new   that

7. There is ....
   you ought to know   very   something   interesting
   about that girl

8. He found himself ....
   bar   extremely   on   disreputable   dockside   an
   the floor   of   lying

9. I have never seen ....
   sailing   such   ship   before   beautiful   a   old

10. My uncle is..
    glass   the   maker   biggest   in   Britain   best
    industrial   and

11. I saw ....
    coming   great   beautiful   a   yacht   big   into the harbour
    white   gracefully   today

12. She found herself ....
    motor-car   face to face   handsome   remarkably   a   with
    salesman   second-hand

13. Patricia was wearing...
    Japanese   a   simply-cut   most   dress   the   beautiful
    silk   made of   I have   ever seen

14. The goats ate ....
    of   half   precious   Robert's   of   vegetables   exhibition
    yesterday

15. Their house is situated on   ....
    old-world   of   city   the   side   green   Salzburg
    mountain   a   overlooking   the   of

16. This floor has been treated ....
    ago   with   months   that   market   plastic   three
    new   on   high-gloss   which   varnish   came   the

17. Richard paid ....
    bull   last   three   year   for   thousand   pounds   Angus
    half   Show   Royal   and   at   a   the   Agricultural   an

18. There was ....
    eyes   his   an   of   kind   grey   expression   old
    understanding   in

34

19. That orchestra is hoping to ....

summer   all   give   in   coming   during   of   concert
autumn   a   country   the   big   the   and   cities   the

20. This car must ....

millionaire   be   certainly   a   the   most   of   order
ever   to   private   expensive   been   made   the   has
one   that

the governess seems to be a
determined young woman

Twenty-nine

The principal verbs in these 25 sentences are in the Passive Voice.
Change them into the Active, and make whatever other changes may
be necessary.

Example: 'He was being told off by the boss.'
Answer: 'The boss was telling him off.'

Example: 'This is believed to be the best.'
Answer: 'People believe that this is the best.'

1. The meal is being prepared by the children tonight.
2. The car was lifted out of the ditch and put back on the road by
   half a dozen helpful farm-hands.
3. Little Basil has been spanked and sent to bed by the new governess,
   who seems to be a determined young woman.
4. Those leaves on the lawn must have been blown there during the
   night.
5. The sailing date's been postponed again.
6. Our garden was judged to be the best-kept in the village last year.
7. No, don't come to the airport with me. I'd much prefer to be said
   goodbye to here.
8. The Vicar was seen by everybody present to be very angry with
   them all.
9. The burglar was alleged to have set fire to the house because he
   was angry at finding nothing to steal there.

35

10. A certain amount of shorthand and typewriting will, of course, be expected from you during your first six months with us, but the work will be arranged so that your knowledge of languages can be put to good use.
11. The week-end's shopping always used to be done by Father.
12. European Governments are to be requested by Interpol, the international police organisation, to co-operate in a search for the escaped murderer.
13. Weren't you told that your luggage couldn't be reclaimed unless the receipt for it was produced?
14. Roger had not been expected to be appointed to the chairmanship.
15. She will simply *have* to be punished for this!
16. The politicians, who had insulted our intelligence with their nonsensical promises, were finally driven off the platform by a shower of eggs and over-ripe tomatoes.
17. Those skirts are now being worn again.
18. I've been offered a ticket for tomorrow's performance of 'Aida'.
19. The number of smokers is said by an official government report to have dropped considerably again.
20. Dick Garnett has been voted by his class-mates to be the student with the best chance of succeeding in life.
21. The promising young actress who disappeared after her successful Athens premiere last month is reported to have been found in the island of Spetsas, suffering from loss of memory.
22. The enemy was soon driven back by our forces on the left bank of the river.
23. The actors were finally shown what we thought of their performance by a barrage of hooting.
24. The Government was unexpectedly defeated last night by a very slim majority.
25. The murderer was betrayed by his accomplices, but only in the midst of a furious gun-battle with the police.

Thirty

What are the feminine forms of these words? (Some will end in 'ess'; others will not.)

Examples: author   widower
Answers: authoress   widow

1. shepherd	6. heir	11. god-father	16. monk
2. bachelor	7. man-servant	12. marquess	17. drake
3. dog	8. horse	13. priest	18. nephew
4. earl	9. tutor	14. murderer	19. magician
5. giant	10. uncle	15. emperor	20. cock

Thirty-one

Form 'confirmative question-expressions' which will be suitable replies to these 25 statements.

Example: 'Mummy, I've just killed a great big wasp that was sitting in the jam-jar.'
Answer: '*Have you?*'

Example: 'I always have a headache next morning if I sleep with the windows shut.'
Answer: '*Do you?*'

(Note: In some cases more than one expression may be possible.)

1. William had three suits made last year.   '_____ ____?'
2. Peter has two beautiful sports-cars.   '_____ ____?'
3. Ronald still had the same little old car, the last time I saw him.   '_____ ____?'
4. They ought to have been a little more understanding.   '_____ ____?'
5. Mary has a dreadful toothache, poor girl.   '_____ ____?'
6. My wife always has a bad headache whenever I want to go through the monthly household bills with her!   '_____ ____?'
7. We used to go there every summer, too.   '_____ ____?'
8. They generally have breakfast out on their verandah in the warm weather.   '_____ ____?'
9. No matter how cold it is, he has a swim in the lake every morning.   '_____ ____?'
10. That actor has his hair trimmed at least three times every week.   '_____ ____?'
11. My jacket has a secret pocket in it.   '_____ ____?'
12. That boy has a very quick brain.   '_____ ____?'
13. They could be there by now.   '_____ ____?'
14. I don't like these apples.   '_____ ____?'
15. He didn't have enough money.   '_____ ____?'
16. She had no time for us.   '_____ ____?'
17. You have some lipstick on your chin.   '_____ ____?'
18. Lucky man! He has three months holiday every year.   '_____ ____?'
19. I had leather patches put on my elbows because the material was getting awfully thin there.   '_____ ____?'
20. Tommy had a sound telling-off yesterday morning.   '_____ ____?'
21. I have at last understood what they are trying to tell me.   '_____ ____?'
22. We haven't much chance of arriving before midnight.   '_____ ____?'

23. That delicate-looking girl over there has the strength of a man. '_____ _____?'
24. Gregory had another garage added to his house last month. '_____ _____?'
25. They might have had trouble over it. '_____ _____?'

Thirty-two

In the blank spaces in these 20 sentences, put *one* or *ones* or *some* or *any*, according to what the context demands.

> **Example:** 'Will you get some eggs on your way home, please? Get new-laid _____, though.'
> **Answer:** '...... Get new-laid *ones*, though.'

1. That hotel looks rather nice. Do you think there is _____ chance of its having _____ rooms free?
2. I hope you have _____ money on you. I haven't _____.
3. No, I don't think he has _____ chance of passing the exam. He hasn't done _____ work at all this year.
4. The majority of the Members of Parliament are men, but there are _____ women, of course.
5. We didn't find _____ Christmas cards that were at all worth buying. The _____ they had were either last year's or absolutely horrible. We'll get _____ when we go to town tomorrow.
6. Cook has grilled us _____ delicious lamb chops. They are so tasty that I don't suppose we'll want _____ mint sauce with them.
7. Would you bring me an orange, Peter dear? There are _____ on the dining-room table.
8. They have a new car now. They bought _____ last month.
9. I'm so hungry I could eat you, too! I haven't had _____thing for nearly thirty hours.
10. Let's go out and get _____ exercise, shall we? It doesn't do us _____ good staying at home all day.
11. Have you found _____ good results in the exam papers you've corrected? The _____ I've done were a mixed bag. _____ were good, _____ were middling, _____ were downright bad.
12. If there is _____ whisky left over after this party, I'll be extremely surprised. But there'll be _____ gin for sure. We'll have a drink and a talk together when they've all gone. That'll be _____ time yet, though.
13. We very much doubt whether _____body could listen to you for more than five minutes without wanting to kick you down _____ particularly steep stairs.
14. _____ inn in Austria is a delightful place.

15. _____ woman telephoned my husband this morning and said she used to be at the University with him. She asked me whether I thought there was _____ chance of his remembering her after so long.

16. Have you heard about Blake's new secretary? She's not only very efficient and very charming, she's also a former beauty queen. That's _____ secretary he's got!

17. Do please eat _____thing more, dear. I'm sorry to keep pestering you, but you *must* get back _____ strength. What would you like? Just tell me. I'll get you _____thing that you fancy.

18. _____ modern paintings are worth looking at, but not many!

19. Waiter, would you please bring us _____ champagne.

20. _____body who can read your handwriting must be a thought-reader with _____ claim to genius.

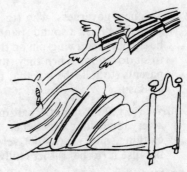

Thirty-three

get up: rise from bed

A number of verbs in English change their basic meanings when adverb-particles (i.e. *up, down, with, by, through,* etc.) are used with them.

> **Example:** get
> **Answer:** get *on*: make progress;
> get *up*: rise from bed;
> get *over*: recover from;
> get *through*: finish or pass (an exam);
> get *round*: persuade by cajolery; etc.

Can you think of *two* special meanings which are created when adverb-particles are used with each of these 25 verbs?

1. make	6. take	11. keep	16. ask	21. whip
2. look	7. sit	12. fall	17. bring	22. cut
3. pick	8. give	13. see	18. let	23. run
4. do	9. come	14. hold	19. turn	24. stand
5. send	10. go	15. put	20. lay	25. set

Thirty-four

Change the verbs that are in parentheses into either the Past Simple or the Past Perfect, according to what you believe the meaning requires.

Example: 'We (to be) prepared for yesterday's rain because the weather forecast (to warn) us about it.'

Answer: 'We *were* prepared for yesterday's rain because the weather forecast *had warned* us about it.'

1. Nancy (to go) to the dentist yesterday afternoon. Her husband (to go) in the morning.

2. When they (to arrive) at the sea-side resort that (to become) so famous, they (to spend) three hours going from hotel to hotel, trying to find a room. They (to have) no luck at all. Every hotel (to be) completely full. John (to blame) himself because he (not to reserve) a room in advance.

3. The new governess, who (to be) a determined young woman, (to give) little Basil a sound spanking and (to send) him to bed because he (to put) a drawing-pin on the seat of a chair that she (to be going) to sit down on. When they (to hear) about it the next morning, his parents (to tell) the girl that they (to approve) of what she (to do) to Basil.

4. We (to go) through the salt-mines of Salzburg yesterday. It (to be) a very interesting experience. The Consul (to tell) us to wear warm clothing, and we (to be) very glad that we (to take) his advice, because it (to be) rather chilly in the great caves.

5. When Peter (to arrive) at London Airport yesterday, he (to be) without luggage. A revolution (to break out) in the country in which he (to work) for four years, and he (to be advised) to leave as quickly as he could. He (not even to have) time to pack a bag. His friends (to rush) him to the airport and (to bundle) him on to a plane. His name, they (to tell) him, (to be) on the list of people who were to be shot by the revolutionaries. He (to be) very grateful to them, for they obviously (to save) his life. He (not to mind) at all about being without luggage.

6. The clock (to strike) four as Mary (to reach) her flat. She (to light) a final cigarette and (to sit) at her dressing-table, thinking of the party she (to leave) an hour before. She would have been home earlier but she (to have) difficulty in finding a taxi at that late hour. Reflecting that if she (not to go) to bed quickly she would feel terrible at work the next day, she (to put) down her cigarette, (to undress) quickly and (to get) into bed. She (to fall) asleep at once. At that moment, the cigarette which she (to put) down but (to forget) to put out, (to drop) from the side of the ash-tray and (to

burn) a hole in the dressing-table cloth. Upon waking some hours later, Mary (to find) that the cigarette not only (to burn) a hole in the cloth, it also (to make) an ugly mark on the wood.

7. Frederick (to come) unexpectedly to see me last night. I (to be) very glad to see him for we (not to see) each other for quite a long time. I (to sit) him down and (to ask) him what he would like to drink. He (to say) whisky, please. There (not to be) much whisky left, but I (to think) there might probably be enough. We (to sit) exchanging news for the next hour or so. Slowly but surely we (to finish off) the bottle of whisky. Then he (to leave). He hardly (to go) when Patrick (to arrive). I (to sit) him down and (to ask) him what *he* would like to drink. He (to say) whisky, please! I (to have to) apologise and explain that there (to be) no whisky left, because Frederick and I just (to finish) it off. I (to have), however, plenty of gin. He (to say) that gin would be very nice.

8. I remember very well the first time we (to share) a room. It (to be) in Haifa just after the war. The town (to be) very full because of a convention that (to begin) a few days before, and it (to be) quite impossible to get a room to oneself. I (to be relieved), however, by the appearance of my room-mate. He (to be) a quiet, reserved type of man, with a nice smile. It (to be) in the middle of the night that he (to stop) being so quiet. A terrible scream from his bed (to make) me jump out of mine in terror. He obviously, I (to see) at once, (to be) in the grip of some dreadful nightmare. I (to shake) him awake, though he (to continue) to tremble for some time. He then (to tell) me that he (to be released) from a concentration camp only five months before and there (to be) few nights since then without a nightmare. His pyjama jacket (to fall) open at this moment and I (to see) hundreds of scars criss-crossing his chest. He (to be whipped) terribly, I (to realise), and I (to understand) something of why he (to have) those nightmares.

9. Bill (to leave) his house at his usual time. He (to hurry) over break-fast because he (to get up) later than usual. Because of his hurry, he (to forget) two things as he (to leave) the house. He (not to say) goodbye to his wife and he (not to take) his umbrella with him. He (to realise) this as he (to get) on to the bus. He (to arrive) at his office half an hour later. The first thing he (to do) (to be) to telephone to his wife. He (to say) that he (to be) sorry that he (to forget) to say goodbye to her. He also (to say) he (to be) angry with himself for not taking his umbrella because the radio (to say) the night before that it would rain.

10. In May last year, Paul (to win) a big prize in the National Lottery, part of which (to be) a house. Until then he (to be) rather poor, and so he (to be) overjoyed with his good fortune. He (to set aside) some money for new clothes, a long holiday, and so on, and (to invest)

the remainder. He (to learn) wisdom from the sad case of Harris who (to win) a similar prize two years before and (to spend) all the money within nine months.

Thirty-five

Here are 25 adjectives. Can you give two synonyms (or near-synonyms) for each of them?

> **Example:** delightful
>
> **Answer:** pleasing
> enjoyable

1. fat	6. angry	11. heroic	16. unhappy	21. frank
2. calm	7. cruel	12. severe	17. ancient	22. chief
3. rich	8. final	13. united	18. exciting	23. vicious
4. evil	9. acute	14. clever	19. suitable	24. obvious
5. fast	10. usual	15. anxious	20. tedious	25. perfect

Thirty-six

Here are five groups of ten adjectives. Those on the right may be used as near-synonyms of those on the left, but their order has been deliberately mixed. Unmix this order by saying which may be used as near-synonyms of each. (Examine each group separately.)

> **Example:** 1. pale   6. paltry
> 2. contemptible   7. parched
> 3. arid   8. wan
> 4. unfair   9. chief
> 5. paramount   10. unjust
>
> **Answer:** 1. pale   8. wan
> 2. contemptible   6. paltry
> 3. arid   7. parched
> 4. unfair   10. unjust
> 5. paramount   9. chief

GROUP A
1. persuasive   6. bad-tempered
2. irritable   7. tranquil
3. reckless   8. convincing
4. annoying   9. daring
5. peaceful   10. irritating

GROUP B
1. biased   6. noble
2. particular   7. passive
3. pathetic   8. prejudiced
4. aristocratic   9. fussy
5. apathetic   10. touching

42

GROUP C 1. touchy
2. famous
3. infamous
4. obscure
5. unrivalled

6. unknown
7. peerless
8. irritable
9. wicked
10. renowned

GROUP D 1. astute
2. judicious
3. immaculate
4. legal
5. phlegmatic

6. spotless
7. unemotional
8. prudent
9. penetrating
10. judicial

GROUP E 1. magnificent
2. outstanding
3. overcast
4. miserable
5. agonising

6. excruciating
7. downcast
8. eminent
9. splendid
10. cloudy

Thirty-seven

23. rogue

Study the vowel-sounds and diphthongs of these eight words:

show, thirst, led, fee, more, got, sit, plunge.

Write the eight words at the top of separate columns.

Now study these 50 words and arrange them so that all those containing the same vowel or diphthong sound will be in one or other of these eight columns.

1. law	11. kit	21. gnaw	31. dove	41. some
2. road	12. cough	22. dog	32. blood	42. comb
3. murk	13. hurt	23. rogue	33. ton	43. floor
4. creep	14. firm	24. rich	34. cloth	44. chips
5. cream	15. ward	25. pitch	35. ate	45. chalk
6. crisp	16. word	26. peach	36. worse	46. groan
7. crept	17. world	27. said	37. bread	47. shown
8. leant	18. slit	28. monk	38. sew	48. shone
9. pea	19. trough	29. ought	39. crow	49. this
10. heap	20. seat	30. son	40. salt	50. hiss

43

Thirty-eight

Read the following passage carefully. Then decide which of these ten words would most suitably fill the blank spaces. If you feel that in some cases a space would be best left blank, leave it blank.

a enough every his some that the their this your

'Go round to _____ grocer's,' she said, 'and buy me _____ cheese.'
'What! _____ whole one?' Peter exclaimed.
'Yes,' _____ mother answered. 'When I was there _____ morning I saw he had _____ few nice little Camemberts, but I hadn't _____ money left. All I could buy was _____ boxes of _____ matches _____ father likes for _____ pipe.'
So Peter got out _____ bicycle. It was _____ pretty battered machine, since it was _____ common property: _____ member of _____ family used it at _____ time or other. And, _____ very morning, _____ boys next door had borrowed it, too, and _____ bicycle was somewhat _____ worse for _____ wear.
As Peter rode down _____ St James' Drive, he began whistling _____ tune he had heard on _____ radio _____ morning. _____ words had gone completely out of _____ head, and, to tell _____ truth, so had _____ melody. But when Peter was whistling he didn't let _____ little thing like _____ worry him!

Thirty-nine

Provide particles (i.e. words like *up*, *over*, *out*, etc.) to complete the items that are underlined in these 25 sentences[1].

1. I always keep a supply of saccharine in the house. It's a useful stand _____ in case we run out of sugar.
2. Poor old Jimmy was completely outplayed in the final. He didn't get a look _____.
3. Ten pence for a wash and brush _____! That's expensive, isn't it?
4. The negligent officer was given a thorough dressing _____ by the Court of Enquiry.
5. Attention all passengers, please! The take _____ of Flight 234 for Beirut has been postponed for another hour.
6. A huge crowd gave the Princess a great send _____ when she left on her tour of Canada.
7. The failure of the prototype was a disastrous set _____ in our plans for the development of a new type of machine.
8. The President said that he could not ignore the build _____ of forces that was taking place on the other side of the frontier.

---

[1]If necessary, see page 1 again for an example.

9. There wasn't a single ticket left. It was a complete sell____.
10. The messenger was the victim of a hold____ as he was carrying the week's takings to the bank.
11. I thought we had been at cross-purposes long enough, and it was time we had a show____.
12. He was on the look____ for a new job.
13. The new discovery represented an important break____ in the fight against lung cancer.
14. The firm's turn____ was more than doubled last year.
15. How do you like the lay____ of our new factory?
16. That little boy has never had anything new to wear. He has always had to accept his elder brother's cast____.
17. The judge decided that the accused man was not one of the principal criminals; he was just a go____.
18. The poor man was reduced to eating other people's left____.
19. The policeman gave Patsy such a telling____ for leaving her car outside the Parliament House!
20. Let's share the jobs while we're on holiday, shall we? I'll do the cooking, as usual. Will you do the washing____?
21. The dropping____ of sales this month is rather worrying.
22. How exciting all this is! I've never seen the blast____ of a rocket before—except, of course, on the news-reels.
23. They have interrupted the count____ again. There seems to be some trouble with the rocket's fuel supply-lines.
24. Come on, all of you! I've just bought some new records. Let's put them on the pick____.
25. No, she uses very little make____, really. But she doesn't need to. She has such a perfect complexion.

Forty

Briefly describe each of these 20 things. Imagine that you are speaking to someone who has never seen the thing you are describing, and who needs your description of its appearance so as to be able to recognise it.

1. a deck-chair
2. a radiogram
3. a handbag
4. a teapot
5. an electric blanket
6. a whip
7. a lipstick
8. a pair of skis
9. a zip-fastener
10. a step-ladder
11. a pair of scissors
12. a cine-camera
13. a wallet
14. a television set
15. a frying-pan
16. a hypodermic syringe
17. an egg-timer
18. a microphone
19. a soda-siphon
20. a vacuum-cleaner

I wish y
were her

Forty-one

I'm awfully sorry, but I had no alternative

Complete these 25 sentences with the correct verbal form selected from the four alternatives that are given in italics below each.

Example: I ...... to the cinema last night.
go   went   am going   shall go
Answer: I *went* to the cinema last night.

1. When your brother ......, he will be very tired.
   arrived   will arrive   arrives   is arriving

2. I shall wait here until you ...... ready.
   would be   are   shall be   will be

3. I wish he ...... louder; I can't hear what he is saying.
   will speak   speaks   is speaking   would speak

4. If I had not called a doctor, your friend ....
   would have died   will have died   will die   has died

5. By next September she ...... the piano for three years.
   will have been learning   had learnt   will learn   has been learning

6. I wish you ...... to our party tomorrow.
   will come   were coming   came   are coming

7. We would have helped you if we ...... you were in such difficulties.
   knew   have known   had known   were knowing

8. Jimmy has been a farmer since he ...... the Army.
   has left   had left   had been leaving   left

9. This is the first time that I ...... your city.
   visited   have visited   had visited   was visiting

10. We ...... here since the beginning of the month.
    are   had been   shall be   have been

46

11. Our train is leaving in half an hour, you know. It's time we ......
from here. Come on!
were gone   are gone   shall go   are going

12. With all this work outstanding, I ...... to the cinema last night.
mustn't go   oughtn't to go   needn't go   shouldn't have gone

13. If I ...... Prime Minister, I'd call for a new General Election at once.
am   was   will be   were

14. It's sure to rain soon. We ...... a drop for over a month.
didn't have   haven't had   haven't   hadn't

15. No, we ...... go in there. It says ENTRANCE FORBIDDEN.
don't have to   haven't got to   mustn't   needn't

16. I don't think we should wait any longer. They ...... that we are
expecting them.
may forget   might forget   might be forgetting   may have forgotten

17. Jim, I do wish you ...... so much, dear. You really are overdoing it,
you know.
won't smoke   don't smoke   didn't smoke   aren't smoking

18. Would you please give him this note the moment he ....
arrives   will arrive   is going to arrive   was arriving

19. Susan ...... a wonderful time at that party last night.
ought to have   must have   must have had   might have

20. Jack, you're back again at last! We ...... you for such a long time.
have to see   didn't see   haven't seen   aren't seeing

21. They ...... at least ten minutes ago.
ought to leave   might leave   must have left   should leave

22. I'm awfully sorry, but I had no alternative. I simply ...... what I
did.
ought to have done   must do   had to do   have had to do

23. The week-end's shopping always ...... by Peter.
was doing   used to be doing   used to be done   ought to do

24. Susan, you are so lazy! This job ...... hours ago.
*should finish   must have finished   could be finishing   ought to have
been finished*

25. You looked at me so angrily just then. I was quite frightened. You
.... to kill me.
should want   might have wanted   used to want   would have wanted

47

Forty-two

Read through this passage to catch its general sense. Then go through it again, putting in the necessary punctuation marks and capital letters.

the mists cleared for a moment and i saw looking down at me the hazy outline of a face quickly i tried to adjust the focus of my eyes for the mist was swirling back again i tried to shout a warning to the face look out its just behind you but my words were drowned by the great banks of fog which billowed back over the face and made everything dark again

i strained my eyes to find some light but everything was black i tried to look behind me but for some strange reason i could not move my head then suddenly i stiffened drew a great breath of air into my lungs and stood as still as death listening my limbs began to shake with fear and drops of cold sweat rolled down my face and dripped off the point of my chin a minute passed and then another

gradually i realised that it was moving slowly through the fog it was sliding up behind me i felt a chill on my scalp and realised with a quiver of terror that my hair was standing up on end it slid nearer and nearer

suddenly the fog swirled as it bounded through the air and landed wetly on my neck teeth bit deeply into my flesh and long sharp claws dug into my throat and began to tear it into strips

sobbing with terror choking and frantic with pain i struggled forward through the fog the thing bit deeper and deeper into my neck and throat i swallowed wetness that i knew was my blood i stumbled and fell on my face i closed my eyes and prayed for death

Forty-three

Each of these 25 sentences contains a space which can be filled by one of these verbs:

say   speak   tell   talk   (in an appropriate form)

Choose the verb that best fits each sentence, and then put its appropriate form into the blank space.

Example: a. '...... me an adventure story.'
Answer: Tell

Example: b. 'Come here,' he ....
Answer: said.

1. George ...... Mary she could come.
2. You must ...... what you want.
3. You must ...... me what you want.
4. Father ...... to me yesterday: 'Don't spend all your money at once.'
5. I was ...... not to be a fool.
6. I think we'll have to ...... this over carefully.
7. George knows a lot of stories and he ...... them well.
8. The subject is closed. There is nothing more to be ....
9. I saw the Secretary of the Club yesterday but he didn't ...... anything about it.
10. Mary didn't ...... that the party was off.
11. Mary didn't ...... us that the party was off.
12. I've this to ...... and this only.
13. He's ...... you again and again not to do that.
14. He must be ...... to pull himself together.
15. Shh! I think the King is going to ....
16. Can you ...... me the time?
17. Why do you ...... such awful lies?
18. It has been announced that the Prime Minister will ...... in to-morrow's debate.
19. As I was ......, just before you came in, we need more money.
20. When I meet strangers I can never think of anything to ....
21. ...... up! I can't hear you.
22. Listen, all of you! Will you please stop ...... for a few minutes?
23. People ...... very highly of her as a soprano.
24. And what have you got to ...... for yourself?
25. Don't interrupt when I am ....

Forty-four

Imagine that you are listening to Mr Black talking on the telephone to Mr White. You cannot hear Mr White, of course, but you could guess what he is saying. Make these guesses now.

Mr Black: Newborough Carpet Store.
Mr White:
Mr Black: Speaking.
Mr White:
Mr Black: Good morning, Mr Wright. What can I . . .?
Mr White:
Mr Black: I'm sorry. I thought you said Wright. Well, what can I do for you, Mr White?
Mr White:
Mr Black: Well, we usually have some in stock, but I'm afraid we haven't any just now. We have some very fine Chinese ones, though.

Mr White:
Mr Black: From very large—about 18 feet by 12—to small ones for the hearth—5 feet by 3.
Mr White:
Mr Black: No, they're all of the same quality.
Mr White:
Mr Black: That depends on the *number* of square feet in the carpet.
Mr White:
Mr Black: Ten pounds the square foot.
Mr White:
Mr Black: On the contrary, Mr White. Ours is a very competitive price.
Mr White:
Mr Black: Then I assure you they must have been of inferior quality.
Mr White:
Mr Black: By all means, Mr White. We're open until seven o'clock this evening.
Mr White:
Mr Black: Good. I'll look forward to the pleasure of meeting you at that time.
Mr White:
Mr Black: 127, Fortescue Street.
Mr White:
Mr Black: Oh, very much in the centre of the town. Do you know where St Matthew's Church is?
Mr White:
Mr Black: Do you know the Rex Cinema?
Mr White:
Mr Black: Well, the church is about 25 yards further on, and Fortescue Street is the turning beside it.
Mr White:
Mr Black: Yes, No. 14 stops outside the church.
Mr White:
Mr Black: Yes, it's convenient, I agree. So, goodbye until six o'clock, Mr White.

Forty-five

2. flood

Here are 21 words that represent all the vowel and diphthong sounds in English, except one[1]. (The letters that are in brackets beside them are phonetic symbols.) Write the words at the top of 21 columns.

see	(iː)	*saw*	(ɔː)	*old*	(ou)	*pure*	(uə)
lid	(i)	*put*	(u)	*try*	(ai)	*fire*	(aiə)
get	(e)	*too*	(uː)	*out*	(au)	*our*	(auə)
cap	(æ)	*but*	(ʌ)	*boy*	(ɔi)		
arm	(aː)	*her*	(əː)	*here*	(iə)		
cot	(ɔ)	*day*	(ei)	*hair*	(ɛə)		

Here are 63 other words. According to the way they are pronounced put them in the columns to which they belong. *There will be three words in each column.*

1. can't	17. man	33. switch	49. coil
2. flood	18. small	34. said	50. doubt
3. cough	19. nice	35. death	51. gear
4. slip	20. full	36. care	52. eye
5. fierce	21. spoil	37. doer	53. brain
6. liar	22. wash	38. wire	54. third
7. mood	23. voice	39. mere	55. does
8. world	24. knot	40. last	56. soot
9. cruel	25. crouch	41. shower	57. come
10. plough	26. though	42. food	58. burn
11. yes	27. flour	43. foot	59. grieve
12. hail	28. truer	44. shoot	60. gnat
13. those	29. tyre	45. core	61. knave
14. power	30. prayer	46. suite	62. jaw
15. there	31. bath	47. plaid	63. scythe
16. these	32. knit	48. ghost	

---

[1] The missing one is the commonest of all; i.e. the sound which is shown by the phonetic symbol ə, and by the letters that are printed in heavy type in these words: **a**bove, **a**gain, under, pap**er**.

Forty-six

Change the verbs that are in parentheses here into either the Past Simple or the Present Perfect, according to what you believe is required by the basic use of tenses.

> **Example:** The five-foot snake that (to be found) last week in a crate of bananas at the London Docks just (to be identified) as a dangerous type of tree-boa.
>
> **Answer:** The five-foot snake that *was found* last week in a crate of bananas at the London Docks *has* just *been identified*, etc.

1. William (to leave) last night for Paris where he (to be invited) to lecture at the Sorbonne.
2. The first time I (to see) the Vatican (to be) when I (to be) at the university. I (to go) to Italy one summer with a group of fellow-students.
3. He (to do) a tremendous amount of work.
4. Xanthippe (not to make) Socrates very happy. She (to be) a domineering woman and she often (to beat) him.
5. No, we (not to hear) yet whether they (to arrive). They (to promise) to wire us immediately, so I suppose they (to be held up) on the way somewhere.
6. Her doctors (to advise) her to live, if possible, in a warmer climate. She (to come) here some years ago and (to like) it. So she (to decide) now to come and settle down here for good.
7. I'm sorry to say that they (to decide) to get a divorce. I (to be) with them for several hours last night and I (to do) my best to get them to change their minds, but I (to fail) completely.
8. We (to be) a bit extravagant last week. We (to buy) a beautiful, big Persian carpet for the living-room. Still, it means that all the essential things (at last to be bought).
9. When he (to get) into the train, he (to look) anxiously around to find a seat. Every one (to be) occupied. He (to shrug) his shoulders and (to lean) his weight against the wall of the carriage. It (to be) then that I (to notice) that he (to look) very ill. I (to get up) at once and (to offer) him my seat.
10. Do you remember that about six months ago I (to ask) you to put our marriage certificate into the box in our safe-deposit? Well, I (to look) for it this morning when I (to be) at the bank, but it (not to be) in the box. Have you any idea where you (to put) it?
11. Look at the time! Obviously they are not coming. They probably (to forget) that we (to invite) them.
12. But we can't move house *again*, dear! We (to move) already twice since we (to come) here. People will think we (to go) mad if we *keep* moving like this! And, anyway, what's wrong with the house? You (to be) very pleased with it when you (to find) it. It (to be) you who (to want) to take it.

13. I (never to know) anyone so amusingly absent-minded. Do you know what (to happen) yesterday? He (to have) a black shoe on his left foot and a brown one on his right! And he (to smile) so winningly when he (to be told) about it. On the other hand, I think he (to make) a good many enemies, too. A lot of people (to be) extremely angry with him. Do you know he once (to invite) fifty people to a cocktail-party and then (to forget) all about it? He (not even to be) in the city that week-end!

14. We had planned to reach Zagreb that night but Fate (to decree) otherwise. About thirty kilometres outside Belgrade, the back axle of the car suddenly (to snap) for no reason that I could see. I (to succeed) in getting a lift back into Belgrade without much delay. I (to have to) leave Susan in the car. It (to take) very little time to get a breakdown-truck into action. In fact, the Yugoslavs (to be) extremely helpful and kind. I (rarely to find) such kindness.

15. Patrick (to pass) his final degree examinations this month. He (to be) very relieved because, he (to say), they (to be) more difficult than usual.

16. I (to hear) a rumour recently that the Government may fall soon. There (to be) a good deal of dissatisfaction last month about that steel dispute, as everybody knows, but I (to have) no idea that the situation (to become) so serious.

17. Wilfred (to make) a lot of money with his last book. But he (to work) extremely hard and long writing it, you know. It (to take) him just over four years.

18. For a long time now, I (to long) to be allowed to drive Father's Rolls, but, of course, I (never to have) much hope. You can therefore imagine how surprised I (to be) yesterday when he (to give) me the key and (to tell) me to take over. It (to be) a wonderful experience! In all my life I (never to feel) such joy in driving a motor-car.

19. What a pity that you (to lend) Tomlinson that money, but of course you (not to know). Everybody in the office (to suffer). We all (to lend) him money, but he (never to be known) to repay a debt. So, of course, we (to stop) lending him anything.

20. Ninety girls (to enter) for the factory's beauty contest this year. Gladys Cox (to win) it last time, and I suppose she'll win it again. To the best of my knowledge the company (not to take on) anybody recently who is better-looking than Gladys.

Forty-seven

Here are 25 verbs. Can you give two synonyms (or near synonyms) for each of them?

> **Example:** permit
> **Answer:** let
> allow

1. endure
2. leap
3. look
4. love
5. weep
6. choose
7. hate
8. build
9. suppose
10. injure
11. control
12. rebuke
13. knock
14. use
15. tie
16. say
17. argue
18. annoy
19. reply
20. stop
21. pull
22. soak
23. finish
24. attempt
25. grip

Forty-eight

In each of these 20 sentences, the word *help* and its derivatives are used in unambiguous ways.

Explain their meanings.

1. If you want to lose some weight, Jim, you must start avoiding second helpings.
2. 'God help me!' he murmured. 'I'm such an idiot! I've made exactly the same mistake again.'
3. He gave us a helping hand when we were in trouble.
4. Yes, I know he's a rascal, but I can't help liking him.
5. Did you have any help from anyone with this composition?
6. Don't be away longer than you can help.
7. I do think you could have been a bit more helpful.
8. 'Help! Help! I'm drowning!'
9. I'm very sorry but I just can't help it.
10. Can I help you in any way?
11. We're a bit hard up this month, my dear, so don't spend more than you can help.
12. Give me only a very small helping, please.
13. I'm telling you the truth, so help me God!
14. We're awfully sorry that we were giggling—but we couldn't help it.
15. Would you help me to carry this suitcase, please?
16. Would you help me to some more potatoes, please?
17. Your liver is not in a very good condition at the moment. If I were you, I'd drink no alcohol for a few weeks if I could help it.
18. Your presence was extremely helpful, I can tell you.
19. The helping you gave me would have fed a football team!
20. The whisky is on the table over there and cigarettes are in front of you. Help yourself.

Forty-nine

5. rest

Here are 25 nouns. They can be separated into five groups, each of the groups consisting of words that have some relationship. For example, if five of the nouns were *appetite*, *steak*, *mustard*, *restaurant*, *bill*, they could be grouped together under the general heading of EATING.

Separate the 25 nouns into five groups, and give a suggestion of a general heading for each group.

1. garage
2. wardrobe
3. water
4. study
5. rest
6. sink
7. pupil
8. sun
9. interval
10. petrol
11. kitchen
12. luggage
13. book
14. saucepans
15. driver
16. chalk
17. tyre
18. tailor
19. shorts
20. beach
21. hotel
22. suit
23. apron
24. material
25. speed

Fifty

A. Put the following into Reported (Indirect) Speech.

1. 'Do you think you can manage Thursday?' he asked her. 'If not, when?'
2. 'I don't particularly want to go,' she said, 'but I suppose I'll have to.'
3. Counsel asked the witness: 'Did you, on the occasion you have just referred to, strike your wife?'
4. The employer told his clerk, 'You can have the afternoon off—I suppose, in these circumstances, I can hardly refuse—but I wish you had told me yesterday.'
5. The girl said to her fiancé, 'I hope, when we're married, we shan't have to live with your aunt, because I don't think I can ever like her.'

55

6. 'If that's what you think,' he said, 'I don't wonder you don't trust me. But you're quite wrong.'
7. 'What are you doing here, anyway?' asked the policeman. 'You know you've no right here. It isn't your house.'
8. The man said to his wife: 'I am sorry I cannot go with you tonight. You must tell your sister that my employer wants me for something he says only I can do. I am sure she will understand.'
9. 'Let's wait here till the rain stops,' she said. 'Then we can walk to the station, unless a taxi comes along.'
10. 'Hold it right side up,' said the electrician to his assistant, 'and, whatever you do, don't jerk it or you'll damage the mechanism.'

B. Put the following letter from Mrs Jones to Mrs Brown into Direct Speech and into the first person. (Begin 'Dear Mrs Brown.')

Mrs Jones is obliged for Mrs Brown's kind enquiries regarding the health of her husband. She regrets, however, that she has not heard anything of Mr Brown's intentions with regard to compensation for the injuries which Mr Jones sustained in the accident for which, as both he and Mrs Jones are convinced, Mr Brown was responsible. In view of the cordial relations that have hitherto existed between them, Mrs Jones would like to assure Mrs Brown that neither she nor her husband desires to resort to legal process, but they both feel that, failing some assurance from Mr Brown, they will have no other alternative. Mrs Jones adds that her husband's recovery is being delayed, and her anxiety increased, by the worry caused by Mr and Mrs Brown's silence on this point.

C. Put the following passage into Direct Speech (beginning: 'How long do you think it will take you . . . ?').

He wanted to know how long the builders' men thought it would take them to finish repairing the roof. Was there any likelihood of their having done it by the next day? He didn't think the fine weather they had been having could last much longer. His wife, who had a flair for weather, forecast that the wind would drop. That generally meant rain; and once the weather broke they wouldn't, of course, be able to touch the roof. Neither he nor his wife could bear the thought that water might seep in on their newly-painted ceilings.

D. Put the following passage into Direct Speech, as you might expect to find it in a play. (Begin: *Mr Smith* (*in an impatient shout*): Do hurry up!)

Mr Smith shouted impatiently to his wife to hurry up. They were already late and if they didn't arrive before the curtain went up they wouldn't be allowed in. He wondered why it was that women could never be ready in a reasonable time.

    Mrs Smith replied that she would be down in a minute. She added indignantly that she had had a busy day, and he must not imagine that she just sat about waiting for him to come home. In any case she didn't really have anything to wear. Should she put on her old green dress or her old red one?

Mr Smith, bursting with irritation, answered that it didn't matter. She could keep her coat on if necessary, couldn't she? What *did* matter was to get there quickly.

Fifty-one

Here are another 25 pairs of words that are often confused. Make sentences to show that you understand the difference in their meanings.

1. councillor
   counsellor
	9. practise
	   practice
		17. polite
		    political

2. irreverent
   irrelevant
	10. pail
	    pale
		18. misused
		    disused

3. corps
   corpse
	11. prophesy
	    prophecy
		19. diary
		    dairy

4. efficient
   effective
	12. literate
	    literal
		20. canvas
		    canvass

5. practical
   practicable
	13. respectable
	    respectful
		21. route
		    rout

6. official
   officious
	14. respectively
	    respectfully
		22. moral
		    morale

7. principal
   principle
	15. stationary
	    stationery
		23. industrious
		    industrial

8. suite
   suit
	16. social
	    sociable
		24. artist
		    artiste

		25. loath loathe

Fifty-two

The blank space in each of these 25 sentences is to be filled by combining the verb in brackets after the sentence with one of these adverb-particles:

> *on, up, down, out, in, by, over, through*

In some cases the particle must come before the given verb and in some cases after.

Example: a. 'It's cold outside. You'd better put on your .... (pull)
   Answer: pullover

Example: b. At the ...... of his career he had little success. (set)
   Answer: outset

1. The ...... of this disease is marked by acute fever. (set)
2. There was a serious ...... of cholera. (break)
3. The ...... for tomorrow's weather is not very promising. (look)
4. There is some sort of ...... between the two firms. (tie)
5. Being made a clerk instead of manager was quite a ...... for him. (come)
6. The ...... of their discussion was negative. (come)
7. We can avoid going through the town by taking the .... (pass)
8. Everybody was very tired, so the party was a complete .... (wash)
9. We had a most awkward ...... on the road to Carlisle. (break)
10. He had a slight stomach .... (set)
11. The ...... washed away the road. (pour)
12. The great scientific ...... of this century was probably the splitting of the atom. (break)
13. The commander stationed an extra ...... to watch for ice-bergs. (look)
14. There was an indignant ...... against the new regulations. (cry)
15. He was very depressed over the ...... of his marriage. (break)
16. It always takes some time to learn the ...... of a new firm (set)
17. Many of the employees are new. This firm has a large ...... of staff each year. (turn)
18. Drink was his .... (fall)
19. He made a lot of money on a small capital .... (lay)
20. His total ...... was £1,000 a year. (come)
21. Three guards were injured in the ...... from the prison. (break)
22. Only £200 was stolen in the ...... at the bank last night (hold)
23. The ...... of this factory is increasing. (put)
24. A further disaster in the kitchen that day was the ...... of water from the sink. (flow)
25. He is limited to a daily food ...... of 1,000 calories. (take)

Fifty-three

first . . . attempt to climb Mount Everest

There are 25 words below, in capital letters. Each one is followed by two sentences with blank spaces. Fill these blank spaces with the forms of the words that the sentences require.

Example: WRITE
a. The ...... of this letter can't spell.
b. Are you interested in ...... as a career?

Answer: a. writer   b. writing

1. BOY
   a. Don't let his ...... appearance fool you. He's a determined young man.
   b. He spent most of his ...... in the Highlands.

2. APPLY
   a. He's the best ...... for the job.
   b. I can't find his ...... form.

3. SUCCEED
   a. He's always worked hard, but he's never been a ....
   b. That was the first ...... attempt to climb Mount Everest.

4. REAL
   a. Poor man. He's completely out of touch with ....
   b. What is needed is a more ...... approach to the problem.

5. FRIEND
   a. No one wants to ...... someone like her.
   b. He was so ...... I finally gave up trying to talk to him.

6. PAY
   a. The instructions say 'This account is ...... at the local post office.'
   b. This is the last ...... we have to make to the hire-purchase company for the car.

59

7. PLEASE
   a. It's a ...... to do business with that firm.
   b. They live in a small but ...... house in the suburbs.

8. POSSESS
   a. His wife is one of those ...... females. He can never go anywhere without her.
   b. It's really not possible to take all your ...... with you on a short holiday!

9. ACCEPT
   a. How many ...... have you had from the people you invited to the conference?
   b. Such a poorly written dissertation is not considered ...... for a diploma.

10. DECIDE
    a. The jury wasn't able to reach a ....
    b. No one was able to give him a ...... answer.

11. RECEIVE
    a. We met one of the Astronauts at the ...... at our embassy yesterday.
    b. If you don't put enough stamps on the envelope the ...... will simply have to pay double.

12. CHOOSE
    a. Beggars can't be ....
    b. Just take your ......, ladies and gentlemen. They're all the same price.

13. SHAME
    a. I don't think I have ever seen such ...... behaviour.
    b. He is ...... of what he has done.

14. APPEAR
    a. It is becoming more and more ...... that the government has lost the confidence of the nation.
    b. The ...... of a five-pound note from my desk suggests that we have a thief in the house.

15. PERFECT
    a. Your job as inspector in this factory is to make sure that no ...... product is allowed to reach a customer.
    b. Yes, I enjoy working as his secretary, but he is such a ...... that it's a bit exhausting!

16. SENSE
    a. Great God! What ...... are you talking now?
    b. It is a very low, evil and ...... newspaper.

60

17. CLEAN
    a. No, I don't think I can wash that jacket. It will have to go to the ....
    b. One should never touch food with ...... hands.

18. VALUE
    a. They say there may be a ...... of the currency soon.
    b. This jewel is not just extremely valuable, it is ....

19. HELP
    a. He was so funny that I was ...... with laughter most of the time he was speaking.
    b. After all we have done for you, I'm surprised that you are so ...... to us, in our own troubles.

20. HEAD
    a. You shouldn't lean out of a railway-carriage window like that. You may be ...... by a passing train, and that wouldn't be very pleasant, would it?
    b. No, if I'm going to drive home I'd better not have any more of this wine. It's rather ....

21. OWN
    a. He's lost some vital papers, poor chap, and he's finding it difficult to prove ...... of the property.
    b. Poor Mary was ...... by her father, and generally treated rather badly.

22. ARGUE
    a. Why are you always so obstinate and ......?
    b. Well, that's a very ...... point, you know. Philosophers have been discussing it for a long time.

23. BELIEVE
    a. No, I disagree with you. I have a strong ...... in his honesty.
    b. There were a lot of atheists and similar ...... at the meeting.

24. UNDERSTAND
    a. We're awfully sorry about what has happened. The whole thing has been caused by a most unfortunate ......
    b. No wonder that Judge is an ...... person. He had troubles himself in his early life.

25. FIT
    a. I don't think he quite behaved himself as ...... an Ambassador, do you?
    b. Jack came off very well in his physical ...... tests yesterday.

Fifty-four

Here are 20 more pairs of words that frequently occur together in English, joined by *and*. Say again which is the order in which they are generally used, and put them into sentences that will illustrate their meanings or uses.[1]

1. chips
   fish
	8. dry
	   high
		15. shoulders
		    head

2. prim
   proper
	9. pros
	   cons
		16. tear
		    wear

3. buried
   dead
	10. cock
	    bull
		17. weather
		    wind

4. spick
   span
	11. steak
	    kidney
		18. dried
		    cut

5. cat
   dog
	12. song
	    dance
		19. blood
		    flesh

6. eggs
   ham
	13. fast
	    hard
		20. far
		    wide

7. bricks
   mortar
	14. by
	    large	

Fifty-five

Here are another 25 English proverbs—with one word missing. Can you again supply the missing word,[2] and say what the proverb means?

1. It's the last _____ that breaks the camel's back.
   lashing   sack   straw

2. The leopard cannot _____ its spots.
   change   hide   sell

3. Life is not all beer and _____.
   enjoyment   company   skittles

4. Little pitchers have big _____.
   ears   mouths   capacities

5. That is all my _____ and Betty Martin.
   brother   eye   foot

6. Big fleas have little _____.
   troubles   families   fleas

---

[1] If necessary, see page 7 again for an example.
[2] If necessary, see page 25 again for an example.

7. A _____ child dreads the fire.
   lonely   *fearful*   *burnt*

8. Old birds are not caught with _____.
   chaff   *candy*   *crumbs*

9. The child is _____ of the man.
   afraid   *father*   *descendant*

10. The cobbler should stick to his _____.
    last   *first*   *cobbling*

11. Don't _____ your chickens before they are hatched.
    count   *sell*   *cook*

12. It's no use crying over _____ milk.
    spilt   *curdled*   *tinned*

13. Every _____ has his day.
    saint   *dog*   *prophet*

14. The _____ bird catches the worm.
    early   *hungry*   *late*

15. Even a _____ will turn.
    statue   *worm*   *Prime-Minister*

16. All work and no play makes Jack a _____ boy.
    rich   *clever*   *dull*

17. Take time by the _____.
    hand   *nose*   *forelock*

18. There's many a _____ between cup and lip.
    slip   *smile*   *tooth*

19. There's no smoke without _____.
    warmth   *fire*   *matches*

20. You can't make a silk purse out of a sow's _____.
    ear   *dreams*   *bristles*

21. There's no royal road to _____.
    happiness   *heaven*   *learning*

22. Rome was not _____ in a day.
    designed   *built*   *destroyed*

23. When poverty comes in at the door, _____ flies out of the window.
    happiness   *love*   *understanding*

24. One _____ does not make a summer.
    swallow   *heatwave*   *swim-suit*

25. You can't make an omelette without _____ eggs.
    buying   *breaking*   *fresh*

Fifty-six

Sometimes, in written English, it is better to replace the verb 'to get' by some other verb, or to omit it altogether. Rephrase these 20 sentences without using *get* or *got*. (In some cases it can be omitted altogether, but in others it must be replaced by some other verb.)

Example: 'I've *got* a terrible headache.'
Answer: 'I have a terrible headache.'

1. She'll get such a shock when she sees how much washing-up there is to do.
2. It took him a long time to get over his illness.
3. Would you run and get me a paper, please?
4. I must really get this tooth taken out.
5. We didn't get back till after midnight.
6. I must get myself a new pair of shoes.
7. Goodness knows how you got round your father to give his permission for this!
8. Williamson's got ten years for that robbery.
9. Would you get me a coffee, please, my dear?
10. Peter got an 'A' in all subjects, in the exams.
11. Do take a coat with you. You'll get pneumonia otherwise. It's awfully cold today.
12. Bob's got himself appointed Secretary of the Club!
13. I've got to finish this before I go to bed.
14. How on earth did that shoe get on top of the piano?
15. Have you got a present for your mother?
16. It took me a long time to get through that book.
17. He's been in bed for several months, but he's just beginning to get about again, with a stick.
18. Peter's French is not terribly good, but he does manage to get by.
19. Have you got what he has been trying to tell you?
20. What sort of get-up are you going to wear for the fancy-dress ball?

Fifty-seven

It's three hundred and ten miles from here

Form questions to which these 25 sentences could be the answers. The information that is particularly required is shown by the words in italics. (Imagine that someone has spoken and you did not hear these particular words. You are now asking what they were.)

Example: a. '*Madeleine* laughed.'
   'Who laughed?'
Example: b. 'Madeleine *laughed*.'
   'What did Madeleine do?'
Example: c. 'Madeleine laughed at *her brother*.'
   'Who(m) did Madeleine laugh at?'

1. It's *three hundred and ten* miles from here.
2. It's *three hundred and ten miles* from here.
3. She was panting *because she had run up the stairs*.
4. She *was panting*.
5. That is *the Prime Minister's* house.
6. *That* is the Prime Minister's house.
7. *Polly* kissed Bob on the end of his nose.
8. Polly *kissed Bob on the end of his nose*.
9. Polly kissed *Bob* on the end of his nose.
10. Polly kissed Bob *on the end of his nose*.
11. Polly *kissed* Bob.
12. *Jackie and Susan* won the second race.
13. Jackie and Susan won the second race *yesterday*.
14. Jackie and Susan won the second race *at Canterbury*.
15. Jackie and Susan won *the second race*.
16. Jackie and Susan won the *second* race.
17. *You* are going to be my partner next time.
18. You are going to be *my partner* next time.
19. You are going to be *my* partner next time.
20. You are going to be my partner *next time*.
21. *The governess* spanked Basil with her hair-brush.
22. The governess *spanked* Basil *with her hair-brush*.

23. The governess spanked *Basil* with her hair-brush.
24. The governess spanked Basil with *her hair-brush.*
25. The governess spanked Basil with *her* hair-brush.

Fifty-eight

Here is another test of your ability to *assimilate* the full meaning of something that you read.

What to do:
i.   Read each piece once—ONLY ONCE.
ii. Cover the piece in some way, and read the sentences *a, b, c, d* below.[1] Only *one* of these is correct.
iii. Decide which of these four is the correct one. *Do not cheat by looking back at the piece before you make your decision.*[2]

1. The old man opened the door of the humble cottage and showed them inside. Its single room was lit by a smoky oil-lamp which stood on a table in the middle of the hard mud floor. Two wooden couches, covered with sheep-skins, stood against a wall. A fire burned brightly on the hearth.

   a. The single room of the cottage was lit by the fire on the hearth.
   b. Its floor was covered with sheepskins.
   c. An oil-lamp was burning brightly.
   d. The floor of the cottage was of hard mud.

2. The old woman shook her head. 'No, sir, no one is a nuisance to us. God has taught us how to live in happiness, although we are poor people. And so you are most welcome to share the little that we have. And now, excuse me, while I prepare the supper.'

   a. The old woman excused herself for being a nuisance.
   b. They were unhappy because they were so poor.
   c. The preparation of supper was not a nuisance.
   d. Though poor, they lived quite happily.

3. Old Mr Jenkinson knew no other language save his own but, with the dignified self-confidence which had always characterised him, he made his way easily about the foreign ship. When the bell announced the serving of lunch on his first day on board he found the number of his table from the list outside the dining-room and went straight to it while many of the other passengers crowded helplessly round the chief steward waiting to be told where their tables were.

---

[1] If you can get somebody to read everything to you, *so that you test your ear too*, the exercise will be even more valuable.
[2] If necessary, see page 14 again for an example.

66

a. The chief steward personally told Mr Jenkinson where his table was.

b. Many of the other passengers crowded round Mr Jenkinson's table.

c. Mr Jenkinson found his table himself, without any help.

d. All the other tables were already occupied.

4. One of the ship's officers asked Mr Jenkinson, a little later in the day, whether he had found any acquaintances on board.

The old man shook his head. 'The only person I've met is my table-companion,' he said. 'I think he's French. His name is Bonappetit.'

'That is not a name,' said the officer gently. 'It is a French expression that means "good appetite".'

'Oh,' said Mr Jenkinson quietly. 'I have been very foolish, I see.'

a. The ship's officer hoped that Mr Jenkinson had a good appetite.

b. Mr Jenkinson had not known the meaning of 'Bon appétit'.

c. His table-companion was only one of the acquaintances that Mr Jenkinson had found on board.

d. Mr Jenkinson said he was foolish to have such an appetite.

5. The young man lay on the top of his bed in the small Vienna hotel, and relaxed. He had been very lucky, he realised. He was free—for the time being. He wondered how long he would remain free. A day or two, at the most. The whole Austrian police force would be alerted by now. And with his own passport he could not cross the frontier.

a. The young man did not think he would be free for long.

b. His hotel was not far from the frontier.

c. He could not cross the frontier because he had lost his passport.

d. The police had surrounded his hotel.

6. Charles gazed over the rim of his glass at the girl who was sitting with two older people—her parents, he assumed—at a table a few yards away. They looked like middle-class English tourists. The girl was about twenty years old, brunette, and very beautiful. She was watching the dancers with a half-bored, half-wistful expression.

a. Two English tourists were gazing at a girl who was sitting a few yards away from them.

b. The girl was a beautiful dancer.

c. Charles was wearing glasses.

d. The girl was sitting with two other people.

7. Gwen and he had been married three weeks before. A few days after their wedding she had had a telegram from home saying that her mother was ill. She had flown at once to London. He had been unable to go with her, for he was a teacher at the Parker Institute

and it was the middle of the summer term. So he had stayed alone, spending most of his spare time at his club because the emptiness of their flat depressed him.

a. He had flown to London with Gwen because he did not want to stay alone in their flat.
b. He did not want to go to London in the middle of the summer.
c. He could not leave the Institute in the middle of a term.
d. He was depressed because he was still a teacher at the Parker Institute.

8. Peter went to the door and opened it. The postman handed him a registered package. 'Sign here, please, sir,' he said, and handed Peter a ball-point pen and an open book. Peter signed his name. He felt in his pockets for a five penny piece. His pockets were empty. 'Wait a moment, please,' he said, and went to the kitchen. His wife usually kept some change in a pot on the mantel-piece.

a. Peter hoped he might find five pence in the kitchen.
b. The cost of the delivery was five pence.
c. Inside the package was a ball-point pen and a book.
d. The postman had brought a registered package from Peter's wife.

9. Richard went into the kitchen and shut the door. He rubbed his hands together purposefully. He took a frying-pan from its hook and put it on a table. He opened the refrigerator and took out a packet of butter and the plate with the raw meat-balls that he had rolled into shape earlier that morning. He switched on the stove, tipped the meat-balls into the frying-pan, and put it on the stove. He then opened the packet of butter and dug out a large spoonful. He dropped this into the frying-pan.

a. Richard usually cooked early in the morning.
b. The meat-balls were ready for cooking when he took them out of the refrigerator.
c. He had bought the meat-balls earlier that morning.
d. He liked to eat meat-balls for lunch.

10. Hadley went up to the hall-porter's desk. 'Have I any letters, please?' he asked.
   'No, sir,' said the hall-porter at once.
   Hadley hesitated for a moment. 'Perhaps you would have a look to make quite sure?'
   'Certainly, sir,' said the hall-porter with a smile. 'What is your name, please?'

a. The hall-porter didn't know whether Hadley had any letters or not.
b. The hall-porter knew that he had no letters.

c. The hall-porter knew that he had some letters, but didn't want to give them to him.

d. The hall-porter hesitated, and then, with a smile, gave Hadley his letters.

Fifty-nine

Change these 25 sentences into their passive forms. Some will require only the simple, basic change, but others will require the more complicated change which uses an infinitive.[1]

1. Someone has already sent for a newspaper.
2. Are you really *giving* me this?
3. Most of us have only glanced through these magazines.
4. He wants to resign, but they have asked him to stay on for a while. They say his presence has a calming effect on the others.
5. We expect that they will be here with us for the wedding.
6. The radio reports that some survivors of the crash are in hospital and out of danger.
7. Your comments did not please him at all.
8. We are turning the room that used to be the nursery into a spare bedroom.
9. Somebody has beaten that poor fellow up.
10. The pot was giving off an appetising smell.
11. What poisoned him?
12. At least one newspaper has said that the Crown Prince is coming to stay in this hotel incognito for a few days.
13. Some people say that it is better to have no jewellery at all than jewellery that is false.
14. Schopenhauer said that a man in love is a man who has lost his senses.
15. An English proverb, on the other hand, says that it is love that makes the world go round.
16. He might have realised his modest ambitions if fate had been kinder to him.
17. People believe that he was kicked out.
18. Do all Scotsmen wear kilts?
19. We're awfully sorry, but we shall have to put you off till next week.
20. Why on earth did anyone send me this?
21. We used to pay her the rent in the middle of the month, not at the beginning as we pay it now.
22. Didn't the Headmaster present the prizes?
23. They think that he was born in this house, not that.
24. They have had to find a much bigger house.
25. Joan and Dick are bringing up their children very sensibly.

---

[1] If necessary, see page 12 again for examples.

Sixty

Here are 20 more colloquial comparisons for you to complete.[1]

1. as ...... as a lord.
2. as ...... as a judge.
3. as ...... as a mouse.
4. as ...... as hell.
5. as ...... as a hunter.
6. as ...... as a sheet.
7. as ...... as putty.
8. as ...... as vinegar.
9. as ...... as a doornail.
10. as ...... as night.

11. as clean as a ....
12. as pretty as a ....
13. as quick as ....
14. as tough as ....
15. as brave as a ....
16. as proud as a ....
17. as ugly as ....
18. as pale as a ....
19. as slippery as an ....
20. as strong as a(n) ....

sea-dog

Sixty-one

Here are 25 more 'head-words', printed in capital letters. Below each 'head-word' there are again six other words. Some, but not all, of these can combine with the 'head-word' to form an accepted compound, *with the 'head-word' coming first in the compound*. In some cases the compound needs a hyphen; in others it does not.

Say a. which words can combine with the 'head-words' to form an accepted compound;
b. what the compound means;
c. whether a hyphen is needed or not.[2]

1. BACK	2. REST	3. SEA	4. SHOE
bone	house	dog	horn
spine	garden	cat	string
chat	hotel	gull	leather
pay	cure	front	foot
earth	light	back	pin
stairs	bed	lawyer	frame

---

[1] If necessary, see page 21 again for examples.
[2] If necessary, see page 11 again for an example.

5. BED	6. EYE	7. SHIRT	8. BARE
fellow	lash	back	faced
man	wash	front	eyed
time	pan	side	haired
cold	opener	sleeves	legged
mail	cover	arms	foot
socks	sore	soap	toothed

9. BLACK	10. WHITE	11. BOOK	12. CARD
guard	wash	mark	board
sentry	top	worm	sharper
back	bottom	slug	blunter
fish	elephant	maker	index
sheep	sheep	keeper	table
leg	leg	dog	pack

13. BRAIN	14. HALF	15. HIGH	16. LADY
storm	clock	footed	boat
thunder	time	legged	radio
wind	wit	handed	bird
wave	crown	brow	killer
ripple	post	light	love
man	caste	ball	hate

17. HEAD	18. MASTER	19. NIGHT	20. PLAY
strong	way	cap	pen
weak	path	hat	girl
road	road	horse	time
way	piece	mare	ground
line	stroke	dark	mate
noise	mind	light	comrade

21. DEAD	22. CROSS	23. COUNTER	24. COUNTRY
heat	question	act	front
warmth	answer	play	back
cold	reply	sing	side
lock	eyed	part	seat
key	footed	bit	chair
letter	roads	pane	man

25. FIRST
   rate
   tax
   born
   help
   hand
   fat

Sixty-two

Here are 40 abstract or material nouns, which, of course, are not normally put into the plural. However, 20 of them have other meanings as common countable nouns, with the consequent possibility of being put into the plural.

Say which are these 20, and make sentences with them to illustrate these other meanings.

Example: beauty
Answer: 'My goodness, there were a lot of *beauties* at that fashion show!'
(i.e. either *women* or *clothes*.)

1. fascination
2. anticipation
3. amusement
4. enjoyment
5. youth
6. fault
7. importance
8. fire
9. laughter
10. awe
11. gold
12. silver
13. iron
14. privacy
15. peace
16. glass
17. land
18. ground
19. rubber
20. plastic
21. milk
22. condition
23. coffee
24. fondness
25. love
26. corn
27. imagination
28. preoccupation
29. kindness
30. scenery
31. spirit
32. air
33. food
34. ice
35. tin
36. wood
37. anger
38. atmosphere
39. residence
40. justice

Sixty-three

In these 25 sentences, fill the blank spaces with the needed adverb-particles (i.e. words like *up*, *down*, *off*, *on*, *out*, *for*, *with*, etc.).[1]

1. Really, Larry, I wish you wouldn't use such expressions in front of me. I wonder where on earth you pick them ......, anyway!
2. I'm not sure whether I can do what you want me to, but let's sit down and talk it ....
3. Nobody really expected him to get ...... that illness.
4. Never give ...... hope, my dear. While there's life there's always hope.
5. Would you ask ...... a glass of water, please, Jim?
6. If I may, I'd like to call ...... you next week.
7. So it's agreed. We'll all go on a picnic tomorrow and you'll call ...... us at eight o'clock.

---

[1] If necessary, see page 1 again for an example.

8. Your father has just left, and he's forgotten to take his umbrella. Take it and run ...... him.
9. It took a long time, but at last the enemy was beaten ....
10. She was almost frozen when she came back. She sat quite still, sipping a cup of coffee, letting the blessed warmth of it reach ...... her body.
11. They're planning to walk all the way to Edinburgh. They set ...... yesterday morning.
12. Elaine dear, wake me ...... in half an hour.
13. If I stay in this place much longer I'll go ...... my head.
14. I hadn't seen him for five years and then I ran ...... him yesterday at the barber's.
15. We've finished ...... the book, so you can keep it if you like.
16. Betty went ...... to the policeman and asked him to stop blowing his whistle at her.
17. Yes, they're extremely nice children. They've been very well brought ......, too.
18. He let ...... his breath as soon as he saw that the aircraft was safely down on the earth.
19. The manager says we can't take ...... any new orders till we've dealt ...... the ones we have in hand.
20. Oh honestly, what an unlikely story, Jimmy! Of course, you made it ....
21. Mr Smith hasn't got a phone on his desk but if you'll hold ...... a moment I'll bring him to this one.
22. Many people are waiting for a place, you know. I have had my name ...... for over a year.
23. You're not sure of the meaning? Well, go and look it ...... in the dictionary. Don't guess!
24. I feel tired, depressed and fed .... I obviously need a holiday.
25. Go to bed at once, dear. You look done ...... and worn ....

Sixty-four

Decide whether these blank spaces need 'a' ('an'), 'the', or no article at all.[1]

1. In _____ quiet, book-lined study, _____ thousand miles away, _____ telephone began to ring. _____ man at _____ desk, _____ man with _____ iron-grey hair and _____ careworn face, lifted _____ receiver. He drummed with his fingers on _____ top of _____ desk as he listened. _____ frown appeared, and grew deeper, on his brow.

   'That,' he said, at _____ length, 'is very bad, Colonel Schroff. He must be found at once. At once, you understand? Get _____ Foreign

---

[1] If necessary, see page 27 again for an example.

Office to ask Vienna to alert their own police. And then get on _____ plane and go and take _____ charge of _____ matter yourself. Nothing in _____ newspapers, though. Take _____ good care of that. We don't want _____ general public to know how inefficient our police force is.'

He listened for _____ moment longer. 'Yes, I see that, but if it ever happens again I'll have _____ heads of all of you on _____ large silver plate.'

2. 'We are sorry to give you this trouble,' said Colonel Schroff, as _____ large black Mercedes left _____ Vienna airport, driven by _____ Austrian policeman. '_____ police of my country were very inefficient. He seems to have given them _____ slip as easily as if they were _____ children.'

'Please do not speak of _____ trouble, Colonel,' said _____ high Austrian police official who had come to meet _____ Air Force plane on which _____ Colonel had travelled. 'It is _____ great pleasure to be of _____ service to your government. *If* we can be of _____ service, that is to say. _____ whole police force all over _____ Austria is, of course, on _____ alert. By _____ tomorrow, every policeman, in even _____ smallest village, will be on _____ look-out for him. And he cannot, of course, cross _____ frontier. So it is certain that he will be found. But _____ Foreign Office of your country spoke of _____ great urgency, of _____ necessity to find him within _____ few hours. And that, I'm afraid, is rather _____ tall order.'

3. After _____ breakfast _____ next morning, Lilian tried to persuade her kitten to come out from under _____ great four-post bed in _____ Ambassador's bedroom. _____ kitten crouched with its stomach against _____ floor and stared impassively at her. _____ wooden sides of _____ bed, reaching down to within half _____ foot of _____ floor, prevented her from sliding within _____ arm's length of it. After _____ few minutes of _____ pleading she went downstairs and found _____ long-handled brush. _____ kitten spat at _____ brush, moved to _____ new position, and crouched down again.

4. About six o'clock on _____ September evening we found ourselves in _____ wild and beautiful valley of Angoraz at _____ foot of _____ pass which leads up to _____ great Plata Plateau. We had seen no reason why two girls should not walk in one day from _____ valley of San Lucarno to San Martino in _____ valley of Castrozza; but through _____ series of unlucky happenings we had lost about _____ hour of precious daylight. _____ most difficult part of _____ journey was yet to come, and _____ sinking sun warned us that it would be impossible for us to reach San Martino. We decided to spend _____ night at _____ Club Hut on _____ Rosetta Pass.

5. When I was _____ child we possessed _____ extremely ugly dog with _____ blackish brown coat, like _____ very old doormat. Nobody at home really liked this mongrel of ours, but over _____ years _____ family had become accustomed to him, whilst we children even took _____ sombre pride in his peculiarities. His temper was sour, he was completely selfish, and he succeeded in dominating _____ entire household. There were _____ chairs in which he did not permit _____ visitor to sit, and _____ cats had to be fed in _____ furtive secrecy when he was not in _____ vicinity. _____ one of his greatest pleasures was to sleep on _____ eiderdown pleasantly warmed by _____ occupant of _____ bed. To achieve this end he had taught himself how to unlatch _____ bedroom doors, and early in _____ morning he would sneak up from _____ kitchen to prowl along _____ corridors and select _____ victim. We frequently forgot to warn _____ guests about this habit of his, and it was only _____ expression of weariness on their faces when they arrived late at _____ breakfast table that reminded us to tell them to turn _____ key in their bedroom doors.

23. ornate

Sixty-five

Make sentences with the opposites of these words.

1. nasty
2. like (*verb*)
3. like (*prep.*)
4. gentleness
5. admit
6. respectful
7. shallow
8. easily
9. debtor
10. contrast
11. hastily
12. beautiful
13. much
14. nearby
15. authentic
16. calm (*adj.*)
17. vague
18. normal
19. superior
20. acute
21. humble
22. cautious
23. ornate
24. talkative
25. sharp

Sixty-six

If we say: 'Patricia made a new dress last week.', we mean, of course, that she made it herself. If, on the other hand, she paid a dressmaker to make it for her, we use the Causative Construction of the verb '*to have*', to express it: 'Patricia had a new dress made last week.'

In the following 20 cases, let us suppose that the subjects are not going to do (or did not do, etc.) the various things themselves, but are going to pay (or paid, etc.) someone else to do them. *The sentences are therefore wrong.* Make them correct by using the Causative Construction of the verb 'to have'.

1. You must clean your uniform.
2. The President has painted the front of his house.
3. I am going to take out this wretched tooth if it doesn't stop aching.
4. Margaret dyed her hair yesterday.
5. The law says that you must sweep your chimneys at least once a year.
6. Will you please polish the brass plate on the door.
7. We ought to make a new one.
8. I think if I put some leather patches on the elbows, this jacket will last for another year or so.
9. They didn't put electricity in their country house last year. They're going to put it there now.
10. They didn't have enough money to put electricity in their country house last year.
11. I have to repair these shoes.
12. Do you examine your teeth every six months? You should, you know.
13. We'll put a stronger roof on the house, and then we shan't be afraid of any hurricane.
14. I'm sorry I'm late, but I've been cleaning my shoes.
15. He's stopped making his sports-jackets. He buys them ready-made now.
16. Please clean up this mess at once.
17. They were forced to exterminate the mice with a dreadful chemical compound.
18. Now that he is in the Navy, he has to cut his hair a good deal shorter than before.
19. I forgot to put air into the tyres.
20. She is going to have to beat this carpet very thoroughly if she wants it to regain its colours.

Sixty-seven

A. The pronunciation of *ough* is very variable, as everyone knows. Can you say how it is pronounced in these 20 words?

1. thought	6. nought	11. hiccough	16. ought
2. drought	7. thorough	12. plough	17. rough
3. borough	8. sought	13. bought	18. though
4. cough	9. bough	14. enough	19. fought
5. tough	10. through	15. wrought	20. dough

B. The pronunciation of *-nger* is also variable. In *finger*, for example, it is ˈfiŋgə; in *singer*, it is ˈsiŋə; etc.

Can you say what it is in these 20 words?

1. longer	8. fish-monger	15. danger
2. hanger	9. money-changer	16. ranger
3. hunger	10. clinger	17. lounger
4. plunger	11. bell-ringer	18. stronger
5. anger	12. banger	19. stinger
6. linger	13. manger	20. scrounger
7. stranger	14. younger	

Sixty-eight

Construct 'question-tags' to complete these 20 sentences, as shown in these two examples:

Example: a. 'Pat'll be coming to our party, ...?'
Answer: '......, *won't* he?'

Example: b. 'He won't be coming to our party, ...?'
Answer: '......, *will he?*'

1. You couldn't lend me a pound, ...?
2. Nobody was late, ...?
3. He used to play a lot of golf, ...?
4. I'm older than you, ...?
5. It's getting late, ...?
6. There's some food left over, ...?
7. There isn't any food left over, ...?
8. She used not to study as she does now, ...?
9. We all ought to pull our weight a bit more, ...?
10. You haven't got a temperature, ...?
11. You also have a lot of difficulty with this type of translation, ...?
12. They had their house re-painted last year, ...?
13. She has to leave now, ...?
14. You shouldn't've told him that, ...?

15. Oh dear! They needn't have taken all that trouble, ...?
16. Tom has a gold jacket on all his teeth, ...?
17. Poor Peter has a lot of trouble with his teeth, ...?
18. You think I'm over-confident, ...?
19. Elaine has been spoken to about that, ...?
20. Barbara has the most beautiful eyes that one can imagine, ...?

Sixty-nine

They had half the police force looking for him

In these 25 sentences, there is a standard or idiomatic expression with one word missing. Below each sentence four words are printed in italics. One of these can be put into the blank space.[1]

Choose this one, and then say what the sentence means.

1. I don't think he should marry yet. He should find his _____ first.
   hands   feet   legs   head

2. For heaven's sake, don't take him so seriously. Don't you realise he is pulling your ____?
   hand   foot   leg   arm

3. Marian is the _____ of her father's eye.
   treasure   apple   orange   wonder

4. They had half the police force looking for him, but he gave them the _____ all the same.
   bird   whistle   escape   slip

5. Necessity is the _____ of invention.
   mother   father   parent   creator

6. Robert hasn't got a very strong character, you know. He generally runs with the _____ and hunts with the hounds.
   fox   hare   deer   rabbit

---

[1] If necessary, see page 31 again for an example.

7. Why are you so down in the _____ today?
   teeth   mouth   ears   eyes

8. He doesn't look very well, I agree. He's been rather off _____ for some weeks.
   colour   health   vigour   fitness

9. It takes two to make a _____.
   double-bed   onion-soup   quarrel   wedding-cake

10. I wouldn't live there for all the tea in _____.
    India   China   Ceylon   Russia

11. You'd better watch your _____ with the manager today. He's in a bad mood.
    step   behaviour   ways   manner

12. We're very sorry, but we can't come. It's quite out of the _____.
    matter   subject   question   topic

13. Finish this job before the week-end? That's a _____ order, that is!
    tall   high   difficult   hard

14. His impudence really takes the _____, doesn't it?
    prize   top mark   cake   biscuit

15. Take care of the pennies and the _____ will take care of themselves.
    others   halfpennies   pounds   dollars

16. Yes, she *was* a girl-friend of mine—once upon a time. But that is all past _____ now.
    experience   history   romance   love

17. Oh dear, my bank balance has gone into the _____ again.
    pink   white   black   red

18. She was rather seriously ill last year but she's in the _____ again now.
    pink   white   black   red

19. That was a _____ letter day indeed, the day Jim was made the manager of his branch.
    pink   white   black   red

20. You need a holiday, I think. You're looking very much under the _____.
    weather   clouds   storm   rain

21. When he retired, he settled down for ever and a _____ in the village in which he was born.
    minute   hour   day   week

22. Look, Peter, let's _____ the hatchet. It's silly to go on quarrelling like this.
    bury   burn   throw away   forget

23. He was as good as his _____. He returned the money on the day he had said he would.
   promise   word   speech   hand

24. Young Richard takes after his father very much. He's certainly a _____ off the old block.
   chip   cutting   piece   bit

25. There is a _____ in the affairs of men which, taken at the flood, leads on to fortune.
   time   tide   opportunity   occasion

Seventy

Each of these 40 words has more than one meaning. Give at least two meanings for each.

1. lap
2. presence
3. coach
4. wash
5. simple
6. suit
7. company
8. degree
9. operation
10. economy
11. ground
12. audience
13. passage
14. member
15. common
16. standing
17. motion
18. experience
19. spirit
20. intimate
21. address
22. patience
23. wire
24. arms
25. single
26. personality
27. initial
28. royalty
29. regard
30. pound
31. craft
32. quite
33. club
34. beat
35. even
36. once
37. very
38. plot
39. wait
40. spell

Seventy-one

In these 25 sentences, the verbs in brackets are again given in one basic infinitive form, which may or may not be correct in the sentence. If this form is not correct, some other form must take its place. If, for example, you have the infinitive (*give*) you may replace it by *to give, gives, gave, giving, given*—or you may leave it as it is in the brackets.

Say which form is appropriate for the meaning of each sentence. (In some cases you may find that two different forms are equally correct.)[1]

1. Customers (be) respectfully (notify) that dogs (be) not (allow) in the restaurant.

---

[1] See page 13 again, if necessary, for an example.

2. I wish you (be) able (come) with us tomorrow.
3. Don't worry! Philip (be) quite used to (drive) in such heavy traffic as this. After all, he (have) (be) (do) it for a good many years.
4. No, Jimmy, don't eat your peas with your fingers. It simply (be) not (do).
5. I should (have) (like) (go) to their party but I (be) not (invite).
6. Would you come with me, please? Your case (be) (go) (be) (take) next.
7. Your car (be) (be) (wash) at this moment.
8. I really ought (have) (have) my hair (cut) yesterday.
9. Since you (have) only just (give up) (smoke), it was very thoughtless of them (smoke) in front of you like that.
10. The baby boy, (have) (be) (abandon) by his mother, (be) (take) to an orphanage.
11. (Have) (enjoy) their stay in Corfu very much, they (decide) (go) there again the following summer.
12. Not (have) (read) the book you (be) (talk about), I (be) afraid I (be unable) (express) an opinion about it.
13. He (have) (be) (go) (stop) (smoke) for years! Only God (know) when he will (do) so.
14. They ought (have) (telephone) (say) that they (be) not (come).
15. This job seems (have) (be) (do) very carelessly.
16. He stopped (type) for a moment and (listen) carefully. Somebody (be) (try) (open) the french windows.
17. My wife (have) (make) me (buy) a new ironing-board.
18. I'd prefer (go) home early but I'd better (go) to their party.
19. Eileen (have) (get) (have) an operation soon.
20. (Need) (breathe) some fresh air, Tom went out on to the balcony.
21. Mary says that she really (have) (have) her fur coat (shorten).
22. Until six months ago, Patricia (be) used to (drive) only in the country but then her husband (persuade) her (try) (grow) used to (drive) in the heavy traffic of the town, too.
23. A metal bar (be) (use) (force) the door open last night.
24. I would (have) (offer) (help) you if I (have) (know) that you (want) (be) (help).
25. I'm afraid I (be) (go) (have) (have) a tooth (take out).

Seventy-two

The initials *F.R.S.* stand for *Fellow of the Royal Society,* and the abbreviation *Blvd.* stands for the word *Boulevard.*

Can you say what these other initials and abbreviations stand for?

1. B.B.C.	4. S.O.S.	7. R.S.V.P.	10. F.R.C.S.
2. Y.M.C.A.	5. N.S.P.C.C.	8. U.K.	11. F.R.C.P.
3. Y.W.C.A.	6. R.S.P.C.A.	9. W.H.O.	12. U.N.O.

13. B.C.	18. P.T.O.	23. Ph.D.	28. Q.C.
14. A.D.	19. B.A.	24. O.H.M.S.	29. V.C.
15. C.O.D.	20. M.A.	25. C.-in-C.	30. M.P.
16. I.O.U.	21. B.Sc.	26. C.I.D.	31. P.S.
17. P.O.W.	22. M.Sc.	27. P.R.O.	32. A.D.C.
			33. F.B.I.

34. Rev.	38. Bros.	42. cf.	46. a.m.
35. Esq.	39. Oxon.	43. et seq.	47. p.m.
36. Ltd.	40. Cantab.	44. viz.	48. anon.
37. Co.	41. Hon.	45. misc.	49. c/o
			50. p.p.c.

Seventy-three

our horse won the race quite easily

Complete the following sentences by using one of the phrases provided after each. Use the form of the verb which is required by the context.

1. The idea of a balanced diet is very difficult to _____ to anyone who knows nothing about food values.
   put through   *take in*   *put across*   *make over*

2. Few people will take the trouble to _____ the question in any detail.
   go into   *give up*   *run down*   *try out*

3. Dieticians have recently _____ suggestions for a complete reform in our eating habits.
   take out   *thrown across*   *put forward*   *make up*

4. They think we should _____ our traditional eating habits completely.
   give up   *take over*   *give in*   *go without*

5. Some people think this would be as bad as _____ food altogether.
   get away   *make of*   *give in*   *go without*

6. Dieticians _____ even deeper prejudices than that, however.
   be in on   *be out of*   *be up against*   *be in against*

82

7. The trouble is that none of us can _____ those who give us good advice.

go up to   *put in for*   *put up against*   *put up with*

     _____

8. I'm sorry to hear that Peter and Dick have _____. They were such good friends.

fall against   *fall out*   *drop off*   *drop out*

9. We must do what we can to help them _____.

do it up   *make it up*   *do it off*   *make it out*

10. Let's start by _____ the general futility of such quarrels.

point on   *throw at*   *point out*   *throw on*

     _____

11. I can't understand how your father _____ that man so quickly. He had deceived all the rest of us.

see against   *see through*   *see to*   *see out*

12. Peter, you're a stupid little boy, you know. Stop _____ like that.

make up   *show off*   *act out*   *do up*

13. The battery needs topping up with distilled water. Will you please _____ it?

look to   *glance to*   *see to*   *watch to*

14. You're joining the class two months late, you know. You'll have to do a lot of extra work to _____ the others.

join in with   *catch up with*   *reach out with*   *make on with*

15. Owing to the bad weather, the garden party was _____.

shout out   *speak for*   *whisper by*   *call off*

16. There was so much noise that it was with great difficulty that we _____ what the speaker was saying.

make out   *make up*   *do out*   *do up*

17. Although he had _____ to a bad start, our horse won the race quite easily.

get off   *run off*   *pick off*   *race off*

18. Yes, Philip is very ambitious. He is _____ for a seat on the Board of Directors.

come in   *leave off*   *go out*   *enter for*

19. Pamela has a nasty cold, but she is hoping to _____ without going to bed.

throw it off   *send it up*   *give it away*   *pass it through*

60%

20. Four yards of this material _____ at £16.

come to   *add up*   *fetch down*   *work out*

83

Seventy-four

Substitute the adverbs *too* or *enough* for the adverb *so* in these 20 sentences, and make whatever other changes are necessary.

Example: a. 'The coffee was *so* hot that I could not drink it.'
Answer: 'The coffee was *too* hot for me to drink.'

Example: b. 'The work is *so* light that I can finish it in a couple of hours.'
Answer: 'The work is light *enough* for me to finish in a couple of hours.'

1. Your essay is written so badly that I cannot read it.
2. Barbara is so rich that she can buy anything she wants.
3. The strawberries are not so unripe that we cannot pick them.
4. The meat was so under-cooked that they could not eat it.
5. The divan-cover was so worn that we could not do anything but throw it away.
6. This hotel is so inexpensive that we can live here permanently if we want to—instead of taking a flat.
7. Peter is so similar in appearance to Gregory Peck that he could easily be mistaken for him.
8. Robert makes his martinis so strong that I can never have more than two if I'm going to drive a car afterwards.
9. I know my wife's habits so well that I can make a pretty accurate guess where she is at this moment.
10. The light in that hotel room was so weak that I could not read by it.
11. I don't know whether he did, in fact, say that—but he is so stupid that he could have done so very easily.
12. You must be wrong. It couldn't have been my sister you saw there. She had so much work to finish that she could not accept any invitations at all last week.
13. We know Alan's movements so well that we were able to be pretty sure where he was all last week.
14. He is so tall that he can reach that top shelf without having to stand on anything.
15. The stones on this beach are so sharp that nobody dares to be without shoes of some sort.
16. No, I don't agree with you. That restaurant is a bit beyond our normal reach but it isn't so expensive that we can't go there once in a while.
17. It was so late that nothing could be done.
18. Madeleine is so kind-hearted that she can give away her last penny, if a beggar looks at her in an appealing sort of way.
19. The room is not after all so full that we couldn't have invited another twenty people or so.
20. She is so beautiful that she could have won any number of beauty-contests if she had wanted to.

Seventy-five

Here are five groups of ten adjectives. Those on the right may be used as near-synonyms of those on the left, but their order has been deliberately mixed. Unmix this order by saying which may be used as near-synonyms of which. (Examine each group separately.)[1]

GROUP A
1. contemptible
2. industrious
3. artificial
4. inadequate
5. petty
6. deficient
7. trifling
8. shameful
9. diligent
10. false

GROUP B
1. tedious
2. tepid
3. calm
4. lower
5. instructive
6. placid
7. informative
8. lukewarm
9. dull
10. inferior

GROUP C
1. lenient
2. harmful
3. inquisitive
4. inexpensive
5. priceless
6. invaluable
7. cheap
8. injurious
9. kind
10. curious

GROUP D
1. negligent
2. mean
3. solemn
4. related
5. ridiculous
6. stingy
7. ludicrous
8. careless
9. grave
10. associated

GROUP E
1. brusque
2. unpleasant
3. slovenly
4. hidden
5. lavish
6. extravagant
7. untidy
8. curt
9. disagreeable
10. concealed

Seventy-six

Put *shall* or *will* into the blank spaces in the following sentences.

1. Don't worry, we _____ have plenty of time to do all that is necessary.
2. I give you my word that my assistant _____ bring you the report before six o'clock this evening.

---

[1] If necessary, see page 42 again for an example.

3. I refuse to be frightened of him. I _____ ask him for the raise I'm entitled to.
4. Never mind how late you are. A nice supper _____ be waiting for you.
5. We _____ have a headache tomorrow if we don't air this room a bit.
6. He is doing his letter-writing now so that he _____ be free to come with us on Sunday.
7. _____ you please close that window, John?
8. _____ I close the door, too?
9. My dear, you look very tired. I _____ get the meal ready tonight.
10. Your name is Spiridakis, is it? You _____ be Greek, then.
11. Every Wednesday evening he _____ go to the Casino for an hour of baccarat.
12. My son is going past the Post Office. _____ he post those letters for you?
13. If ever you do that again, you _____ have a very good spanking!
14. _____ you have another cup of tea?
15. We are anxious that Richard _____ be offered the chairmanship.
16. _____ I ever be able to learn this language?
17. It is intended that, before the end of the month, everybody _____ have received the bonus.
18. If you wish, I _____ help you with that job.
19. I think I _____ go to the club for a game of poker tonight, my dear —if you don't mind.
20. I don't care what the doctor says. On such a beautiful day I _____ not stay indoors like a prisoner.

11. omen

Seventy-seven

Here are 25 nouns. Can you give a near-synonym for each of them?

1. modification
2. mood
3. morality
4. sorrow
5. scarf
6. mutiny
7. neglect
8. destiny
9. noise

86

10. remark
11. omen
12. opportunity
13. penalty
14. peacemaker
15. petition
16. thought
17. foolishness
18. leader
19. cruelty
20. diagram
21. merchandise
22. moisture
23. ornamentation
24. possession
25. magnificence

Seventy-eight

The plural of 'a' varies according to whether it is used numerically or generally. If it is used *numerically*, such words as *two, three, some, several, a few, a number of*, etc., must take its place before the plural noun.

    Example: 'Rene has *a* beautiful dog.'
The Plural: 'Rene has *three (two, some, several, a few, a number of)* beautiful dogs.'

If it is used *generally*, no word at all takes its place before the plural noun.

    Example: '*A* dog can be wonderful company for *a* lonely person.'
The Plural: 'Dogs can be wonderful company for lonely people.'

Rephrase these 20 sentences with the italicised nouns in the plural. Make whatever other changes are necessary.

1. Timothy has just bought *a car*.
2. In this town, *a car* is more trouble than it is worth.
3. Even on *a* very hot *day*, *a church* is usually cool.
4. We shall be away for about *a week*.
5. One can be sure of hearing *a* good *concert* there.
6. Somebody has broken *a mirror* in the washroom.
7. *A mackintosh* used to be made of rubber.
8. May I have *a bottle* of beer, please?
9. Yes, I have had *a haircut* there.
10. *An egg* contains valuable proteins.
11. If *a dog* could only speak, what secrets it could tell!
12. There is *a* beautiful two-hundred-year-old *oak-tree* just outside their front door.
13. If you suffer from insomnia, you could take *a pill* occasionally.
14. I have just met *a* famous *opera-singer*.
15. The new government is planning to build *a motorway* in the north.
16. *A cocktail-party* generally lasts for two hours.
17. *A* Byzantine *ikon* is a beautiful thing to have on the walls of a study.
18. *An alsatian* is *a dog* that usually obeys only one person.
19. I like to take *an apple* to bed with me.
20. *A woman* can often endure pain and hardship better than *a man*.

Seventy-nine

The words in brackets in front of each of these 25 sentences are to be combined in one of three ways:

1. as a possessive phrase;

   Example: (man, hat) 'That hat she is wearing is strange. It looks like a ....'
   Answer: man's hat

2. as one noun followed by a prepositional phrase with *of*;

   Example: (bus, back) 'Shall we sit at the ......?'
   Answer: back of the bus

3. as a simple sequence of two words;

   Example: (book, cover) 'You should make a plastic ...... to protect the book.'
   Answer: book cover

1. (pay, day) We collected our ...... after work each day.
2. (key, car) Did you pick up my ......?
3. (leg, table) Can you fix that ......? It seems to be broken.
4. (book, page) What's that piece of paper on the floor? It looks like a ....
5. (man, job) You shouldn't be doing that, Mary. That's a ....
6. (neck, back) John's got a pain in the ....
7. (leg, John) What's the matter with ......?
8. (work, hour) This shouldn't take us very long. I'd say it's about an ....
9. (lamp, table) It's a bit dim in this corner. You'd better buy a small ......
10. (job, professional) That was very well done. In fact, it looked like a ....
11. (film, war) I don't want to see that film. I can't stomach another ......
12. (story, children) Even though it's a ......, it's quite amusing.
13. (throw, stone) He has very little trouble catching trains, living as he does a ...... from the station.
14. (house, doll) I'm making a ...... for my daughter.
15. (wine, bottle) Will you please buy a ...... for dinner on your way home.
16. (women, magazine) This ...... seems to have been written for rich women only.
17. (television, advertisements) All ...... are too long.
18. (coffee, cup) There are only four cups and five people. Isn't there another ...... in the cupboard?
19. (living, cost) The ...... has risen again.

20. (soap, dish) I have asked you many times not to leave the …… full of water.
21. (side, house) That …… needs a new coat of paint.
22. (hand, whip) What a fool he is! Doesn't he see that he's given her the …… now.
23. (hard-luck, story) One of these days, somebody is going to believe at least one …… that he tells.
24. (shoes, stiletto-heel) The Committee is going to ask lady members to refrain from wearing …… in the new reception-rooms.
25. (clerk, income) I wish I could buy a car like that, but on a …… it is quite impossible.

Eighty

Affirmative suppositions are usually expressed in English by *must*, and negative suppositions by *cannot*. In these 20 sentences, omit the words *I suppose that* or *I don't suppose that*, and rephrase the sentences with *must* or *cannot*.

> **Example:** a. 'I suppose that they are very poor.'
> **Answer:**　　'They must be very poor.'

> **Example:** b. 'I don't suppose they have much money.'
> **Answer:**　　'They cannot (can't) have much money.'

1. I suppose that they are at home now.
2. I suppose that that hotel is extremely expensive.
3. I suppose that your coat is very warm.
4. Listen! I suppose that it's raining.
5. I don't suppose she is more than 20 years old.
6. I don't suppose that you like food cooked in that way, do you?
7. I suppose that you worked very late last night.
8. I suppose that Maurice has taken our umbrella again.
9. I don't suppose that you enjoyed that party much.
10. I suppose that you are wrong.
11. I suppose that you are not right about that.
12. I suppose that she was a very attractive woman.
13. It is such a lovely day that I suppose they have gone out for the day.
14. It's after midnight. I don't suppose that the children are still up.
15. Look at all these mistakes. I don't suppose that you read it through again when you finished it, did you?
16. I suppose that he was born in this village, wasn't he?
17. You say that the humidity reaches 90% in summer! I don't suppose it's a very nice place to live in.

18. She is always nagging at him—and they've only been married a couple of months. I don't suppose he is over-pleased with married life, after all.
19. I've never seen such a luxurious house. I suppose it cost a fortune to build and furnish.
20. From your name, I suppose that you are Armenian.

Eighty-one

... it was difficult to recognise Anthony Quinn

In the appropriate tenses or forms, insert either the verb *make* or the verb *do* in these blank spaces.

1. 'Where is Mary?' 'She is _____ the beds, I think.'
2. Nine times six _____ fifty-four.
3. A glass of burgundy would _____ you good tonight.
4. We must get some new curtains _____.
5. They have _____ him the Chairman of the Board.
6. Have you _____ a lot of work today?
7. Has he _____ that new chair he promised me?
8. They seem to be _____ a lot of changes in their plans.
9. Try not to _____ any noise for the next half-hour.
10. No, we didn't feel like _____ anything else, so we went home early.
11. It doesn't _____ to interrupt him while he's concentrating.
12. Jennifer, this is typed very badly. I'm afraid you'll have to _____ it again.
13. I can't think why you're so angry. I haven't _____ anything wrong.
14. Under that very clever _____ up it was difficult to recognise Anthony Quinn.
15. I think I'll _____ my homework now and get it finished with.
16. She's going to bed. She says she feels a bit _____ up after so much walking.
17. This medicine tastes awful, I know, but it will _____ you well again.
18. I think I could _____ a bookcase out of these pieces of wood.

19. Whatever have you _____ with my scissors, Jim?
20. Did you _____ what I asked you to, Tom?
21. What are you _____ such a fuss about, Peter?
22. I'm not at all surprised that she doesn't want to go with you. She'll just have to be _____ to, though.
23. Oh look! You've spilled some soup and _____ a mess of the carpet.
24. Here are the financial reports, Maurice. We do not want you to have the slightest suspicion that you are being _____ out of your fair share of the company's profits.
25. I have to ask you to _____ me a great favour, Jenny.

Eighty-two

The following 25 sentences are divided into two parts; these parts are printed on separate lines and marked *a.* and *b.* In each case, say what sequences of *a.* and *b.* seem to you to represent correct sentences.

Example: a. that you answer the letter immediately
b. it is important
Answer: *b. a.* (Only this order is correct.)

Example: a. because he was late
b. he took a taxi
Answer: *a. b.* and *b. a.* (Either order is correct.)

1a. to avoid all that traffic
b. there is a way

2a. when he finally got to the party
b. he enjoyed himself

3a. we should find a place to study
b. where we shall not be interrupted

4a. although he is very charming
b. he isn't terribly bright

5a. in spite of the many parties he goes to
b. John is always bright and alert

6a. that he had to go
b. he shouted

7a. he's been in France only two months
b. yet he speaks French extremely well

8a. when they first came here
b. they didn't know anyone

91

9a. who is in town for a few days
b. I had a drink with my daughter's husband

10a. how many students we have
b. can't you tell me

11a. I've re-arranged the living-room furniture
b. to make better use of the space

12a. how many students we have
b. can easily be determined

13a. that you are an idiotic fathead with the brain of a cock
b. is a fact of which I have long been sadly aware

14a. there is a waste-paper basket
b. there in the corner

15a. it's all my fault
b. it's very unkind of you to say

16a. whether he likes me or not
b. I don't care two hoots

17a. she finished the job
b. although she could hardly keep her eyes open

18a. walking in the rain can be pleasant
b. provided you have water-tight shoes on

19a. in spite of the insect-repellent that he had put on his skin
b. he was bitten by a mosquito

20a. so that the car should not skid on the hard snow
b. he bought some chains

21a. to smoke here
b. it is strictly forbidden

22a. to understand his mumbling conversation
b. needs a lot of patience and steady nerves

23a. only with very hard practice
b. you can become a good pianist

24a. only with very hard practice
b. can you become a good pianist

25a. only Tom can play the piano
b. in my family

Eighty-three

Each of these 25 sentences contains a blank space which may or may not need a preposition. Below each sentence two prepositions are shown. Decide whether a preposition is needed, and, if so, which one of the two it is; if not, simply say so.

Example: a. 'He depends _____ us for everything.'
from   on
Answer: *on* is needed.

Example: b. 'We watch the King _____ arrive.'
to   for
Answer: No preposition is needed.

1. I shall be passing _____ Paris next month. I'll come and see you, if I may.
from   through

2. She answered _____ all my questions very frankly.
to   of

3. The poor chap was robbed _____ everything he possessed.
from   of

4. My son is an expert _____ electronics.
for   in

5. We enjoy _____ their company very much indeed.
with   in

6. We amuse ourselves very much _____ their company.
with   in

7. They have converted their house _____ a number of flats.
to   into

8. The meeting consisted mainly _____ women.
of   from

9. The concert had already begun when we arrived _____ the theatre.
to   at

10. May I ask _____ you to do me a great favour.
from   by

11. It was midnight before we reached _____ our destination.
to   at

12. No, plastic is quite different _____ rubber.
from   to

13. Do you believe _____ what he told us?
to   at

93

14. If I go back _____ my mind through the years I realise I have had a very lucky life.
   with   in

15. He has a beautiful house _____ these mountains.
   in   on

16. I met her _____ the Smiths' party last week.
   to   at

17. Is it possible _____ you to help me with this?
   for   to

18. This cottage reminds _____ me of the one I was born in.
   to   of

19. Philip paid _____ the company £25 as a down-payment.
   at   to

20. Mary plays _____ the violin almost as well as her teacher now.
   on   at

21. When she entered _____ the room, we saw that she had been crying.
   in   into

22. At the Rex this week, there is a film _____ the life of Sir Alexander Fleming.
   from   about

23. What is the difference _____ this and that?
   with   between

24. We have lived here _____ the end of the war.
   from   since

25. Do you think that you can cure him _____ that disease, Doctor?
   from   of

Eighty-four

Indicate clearly and fully, in any way that you wish, the difference in the meanings of the sentences in these pairs and groups.

   1a. None of the lights was too strong.
   b. The lights were none too strong.

   2a. What did he say?
   b. He said *what*?

   3a. They were hard hit by the devaluation of the currency.
   b. They were hardly affected by the devaluation of the currency.

94

4a. They saw that he had been punished.
 b. They saw to it that he was punished.

5a. No one did anything that night.
 b. No one did nothing that night.

6a. We wish him to be our leader.
 b. We wish he were our leader.

7a. This is the most interesting work.
 b. This is most interesting work.

8a. My first feeling was one of fear.
 b. At first, I was afraid.
 c. First and foremost, I was afraid.

9a. Rosemary may well be able to sell her car.
 b. Rosemary may be able to sell her car well.
 c. Rosemary may be able to sell her car as well.

10a. He turned up the next day with a wife and several children.
 b. He turned up the other day with a wife and several children.

11a. Sure she is the right person to ask?
 b. Surely she is the right person to ask?
 c. Certainly she is the right person to ask.

12a. The house was sold for £18,000 or so.
 b. The house was sold for practically £18,000.
 c. The house was sold for upwards of £18,000.

13a. Had you met her?
 b. Did you meet her?

14a. They sent a doctor at once.
 b. They sent for a doctor at once.

15a. Shall we ask them in?
 b. Shall we ask them out?

16a. Christopher doesn't shave himself every day.
 b. Christopher himself doesn't shave every day.

17a. Can we afford to ignore them?
 b. Can we afford not to know them?

18a. This is not completely wrong.
 b. This is not at all wrong.

19a. Don't be late, Jack.
 b. Don't be long, Jack.

20a. We tried to make him feel ashamed of himself.
 b. We tried making him feel ashamed of himself.

Eighty-five

burst

Here are five groups of ten verbs. Those on the right may be used as near-synonyms of those on the left, but their order has been deliberately mixed. Unmix this order by saying which may be used as near-synonyms of which. (Examine each group separately.)

GROUP A
1. exist
2. burst
3. seek
4. demonstrate
5. drop

6. explode
7. show
8. fall
9. search
10. live

GROUP B
1. fasten
2. settle
3. smack
4. flicker
5. fetch

6. bring
7. slap
8. tie
9. arrange
10. glimmer

GROUP C
1. wrinkle
2. feed
3. prophesy
4. forget
5. gamble

6. foretell
7. bet
8. crease
9. nourish
10. overlook

GROUP D
1. stare
2. capture
3. glare
4. delight
5. grab

6. take
7. scowl
8. gaze
9. seize
10. please

GROUP E
1. limp
2. injure
3. mature
4. suggest
5. meet

6. ripen
7. imply
8. encounter
9. hobble
10. wound

Eighty-six

Into these blank spaces, put either *a (an)*, *the*, or no article at all, according to what you think is required.

1. I shouldn't trust him so much, if I were you. He has been in _____ prison three times for _____ fraud.
2. Richard has gone to _____ hospital to see his uncle who has had _____ operation.
3. I'm very fond of _____ simple supper of _____ fresh bread, _____ butter, _____ cheese, _____ onion, and _____ bottle of _____ beer.
4. Pamela was away from _____ school most of _____ last month because of _____ illness. She was in _____ hospital for _____ ten days, in _____ fact.
5. No, Timothy isn't up yet. He always lies later in _____ bed on _____ Sundays.
6. _____ rich should help _____ poor.
7. They go very often to _____ cinema but very seldom to _____ theatre.
8. This is _____ tenth time that it has happened.
9. _____ more I see of him _____ less I like him.
10. He is studying _____ political economy at _____ night-school.
11. It's dreadfully late. Let's all go to _____ bed, shall we? We can continue _____ discussion at _____ breakfast.
12. He already speaks six foreign languages, and now he is studying _____ seventh.
13. Can you play _____ piano?
14. There was _____ terrible accident in _____ Drake Street _____ hour ago. _____ lorry collided with _____ bus. Seven people were killed and about _____ dozen injured. _____ injured were rushed to _____ nearest hospital and _____ dead were taken quickly to _____ mortuary of _____ district.
15. You seem to have enjoyed your holiday on _____ Riviera. Are you going there again _____ next summer?
16. We have been asked to help with _____ collection of _____ money for _____ Cancer Fund _____ next month.
17. Look at that revolting spider on _____ bed. Do get _____ swatter and kill it.
18. I met _____ Governor of _____ county prison at _____ Sinclairs' party _____ last week. He told me that he had been in _____ navy until _____ last June.

19. _____ visit to _____ monasteries of _____ Mount Athos in _____ Greece is being planned by _____ young men of this College for _____ next summer. Only by _____ men, though; _____ women are not allowed on _____ Mount Athos.
20. _____ last time I was here was during _____ last week of _____ Christmas holidays _____ last year.

Eighty-seven

Here are 25 nouns. They can be separated into five groups, each of the groups consisting of words that have some relationship. For example, if five of the nouns were *appetite, steak, mustard, restaurant, bill,* they could be grouped together under the general heading of EATING.

Separate the 25 nouns into the five groups, and give a suggestion of a general heading for each group.

1. ticket
2. priest
3. station
4. proposal
5. pillow
6. police
7. garden
8. alarm-clock
9. fine
10. seed
11. nightmare
12. root
13. honeymoon
14. judge
15. picnic
16. flower
17. cell
18. engagement
19. time-table
20. crime
21. ring
22. dining-car
23. rain
24. water-bottle
25. mattress

Eighty-eight

A. Into these blank spaces, put either *It* or *There.*

1. Let's open the windows. _____'s awfully hot.
2. _____ was still the fashion for literary hostesses to give large evening parties.
3. _____'s an anti-cyclone, they say, heading in our direction.
4. _____'s an anti-cyclone they say, which is heading in our direction.
5. _____ does one a great deal of good to walk about a mile every day.
6. _____'s no doubt that he will be elected.
7. _____'s not at all doubtful that he will be elected.
8. _____ was very interesting, listening to those two.
9. _____'s some lipstick on your forehead.
10. _____'s clear that you weren't listening to what I was saying.

B. Into these blank spaces, put either *still* or *yet*.

1. 'Hasn't Roger come home _____?'
   'No, we're _____ waiting for him.'
2. Be careful. This paint is _____ wet.
3. It's going to be difficult to understand this lesson because we're _____ beginners.
4. He failed the examination hopelessly, and _____ I'm perfectly certain that he studied as hard as everybody else.
5. I know it's cheaper than we expected but I _____ think that we should not buy it _____.
6. We have found ten different meanings of this word, and there is another one _____.
7. Do you _____ insist that this restaurant is better than that other one?
8. Elizabeth, haven't you made the beds _____? It's lunchtime and they're _____ unmade! Aren't you ashamed of yourself?
9. 'Are you _____ taking French lessons?'
   '_____? Good heavens, no. I haven't started _____.'
   'I'm _____ far too busy with English.'
10. In spite of your objections, we are _____ determined to go forward with the original plan.

Eighty-nine   *Needs must when the . . . drives*

Here are 25 more proverbs with one word missing. Can you supply the word, and say what the proverb means?[1]

1. Nothing venture, nothing _____.
   have   lose   gain

2. A good example is better than a _____.
   thrashing   rebuke   sermon

---

[1] If necessary, see page 25 again for an example.

3. A man's home is his _____.
   safety   castle   home

4. Let sleeping dogs _____.
   dream   lie   snore

5. Many _____ make light work.
   hands   servants   plans

6. There's no disputing about _____.
   women   tastes   fashions

7. It takes all sorts to make a _____.
   programme   salad   world

8. No man is a hero to his _____.
   wife   valet   employer

9. Everything comes to him who _____.
   grumbles   prays   waits

10. _____ begins at home.
    Charity   Love   Education

11. Half a loaf is better than no _____.
    bread   loaf   food

12. As well be _____ for a sheep as a lamb.
    paid   hanged   prepared

13. More haste, less _____.
    result   speed   perfection

14. The road to Hell is paved with good _____.
    intentions   stones   bones

15. Hitch your _____ to a star.
    dreams   wagon   ambitions

16. Every _____ has his Jill.
    criminal   Jack   cowboy

17. You must know how many _____ make five.
    times   chances   beans

18. It's too late to shut the stable-door after the _____ has gone.
    stableboy   straw   horse

19. A little _____ is a dangerous thing.
    learning   explosive   poison

20. One must draw the _____ somewhere.
    water   curtains   line

21. It's a long _____ that has no turning.
    chapter   lane   visit

22. Needs must when the _____ drives.
    manager   devil   learner

23. Never do things by _____.
    halves   yourself   candlelight

24. No news is _____ news.
    bad   good   no

25. Prevention is better than _____.
    cure   whipping   medicine

Ninety

Briefly describe each of these 20 things. Imagine that you are speaking to someone who has never seen the thing you are describing, and who needs your description of its appearance so as to be able to recognise it.

1. a comb
2. a test-tube
3. a helicopter
4. a piano
5. a glove
6. a fountain pen
7. a waterfall
8. a radiator
9. a typewriter
10. a fireplace
11. an electric fan
12. a chimney
13. a violin
14. a tape-recorder
15. a pair of handcuffs
16. a sundial
17. a toasting-machine
18. a pressure-cooker
19. a church organ
20. a pair of roller skates

Ninety-one

Form questions to which these 25 sentences could be the answers. The information that is particularly required is shown by the words in italics. (Imagine that someone has spoken and you did not hear these particular words. You are now asking what they were.)[1]

1. *Our children* began to climb their apple-tree.
2. *Our* children began to climb their apple-tree.
3. Our children *began to climb their apple-tree.*
4. Our children began to *climb their apple-tree.*
5. Our children began to climb *their apple-tree.*
6. Our children began to climb *their* apple-tree.

---
[1] See page 65 again, if necessary, for an example.

7. Polly was *crying*.
8. Polly was crying *because Hugh had smacked her*.
9. They were *having tea* on the lawn.
10. They were having tea at the *far* end of the lawn.
11. To Robinson, *Jenner* was the nearest human thing to the devil.
12. To *Robinson*, Jenner was the nearest human thing to the devil.
13. To Robinson, Jenner was *the nearest human thing to the devil*.
14. They say that charity begins *at home*.
15. They say that *charity* begins at home.
16. We'll *have breakfast* on the terrace tomorrow.
17. We'll have *breakfast* on the terrace tomorrow.
18. We'll have breakfast *on the terrace* tomorrow.
19. The early bird catches *the worm*.
20. The *early* bird catches the worm.
21. They close *this road* twice a year.
22. They close *this* road twice a year.
23. They close this road *twice a year*.
24. They close this road *twice* a year.
25. I said they *close* this road twice a year.

Ninety-two

Here is another 'one-sided' telephone conversation. You know what Mr Brown says, but you cannot hear what the other (the Hotel Reception Clerk) replies. You may, however, be able to guess.

Mr Brown: Hello! Hello! I want the Hotel Splendide, please.
The other:
Mr Brown: What did you say? I can't hear you very well.
The other:
Mr Brown: Oh, you *are* the Hotel Splendide. Something seems to be the matter with this line.
The other:
Mr Brown: Well, it does sometimes help to do that, but I can't just ring off and try again now because this is a long-distance call. Will you put me through to the Reception, please?
The other:
Mr Brown: What? Oh, you *are* the Reception. Good. I want to book a double room with bath, overlooking the sea. It must be quiet.
The other:
Mr Brown: Oh, for two weeks beginning August 1st. August 1st to 14th inclusive.
The other:
Mr Brown: But you must have some!

The other:

Mr Brown: But surely a hotel of your size could fit in two elderly people at *any* time of the year. Provided it's quiet I don't much mind if it doesn't have a view of the sea.

The other:

Mr Brown: At the back? Oh. Is it quiet there?

The other:

Mr Brown: I see. Yes, I suppose there must be a certain amount of noise at the front from the promenade. Is it a good big room—as big as the front ones?

The other:

Mr Brown: A double bed? Oh no. I meant twin beds in a double room. We are both very light sleepers. We must have single beds.

The other:

Mr Brown: Right up there? I suppose it's all right provided there's a lift. What about the bath? It has one?

The other:

Mr Brown: But we *must* have a bath to ourselves. My wife is not accustomed to wandering along corridors with her sponge-bag.

The other:

Mr Brown: The seventh floor! Oh dear.

The other:

Mr Brown: A private suite! Oh, I see. Of course, put that way my wife won't mind the seventh floor so much. Er—what does it cost?

The other:

Mr Brown: Good gracious! That seems a lot.

The other:

Mr Brown: Yes, of course. And it *is* a private suite. Very well then. Will you please book this private suite on the seventh floor for August 1st to 14th inclusive? Thank you. Good-bye.

The other:

Mr Brown: Oh yes, of course. How very silly of me. Brown. R. G. Brown, 125 Duke Street, South Lampton.

The other:

Mr Brown: No, no. South*ampton* is very far away from where we live. I said South *Lamp*ton, and it is in Cheshire.

The other:

Mr Brown: Of course. Don't say another word. Many people make the same mistake. Quite often.

The other:

Mr Brown: Yes, I agree. They do sound very similar, especially on the telephone.

The other:

Mr Brown: Good. Thank you very much. We'll be arriving in the early evening. Goodbye till then.

103

Ninety-three

Below are 25 words arranged in alphabetical order. Rearrange them into five groups bringing together those which are similar or related in meaning. (Each group will have five words.)

An example of such a five-word group is:
outlook, *view*, *scene*, *prospect*, *vista*.

accident, air, announcement, authority, bulletin, calamity, control, communication, disaster, ditty, domination, flat, hotel, house, influence, lodging, message, melody, misfortune, notice, power, residence, song, trouble, time.

Ninety-four

Write a paragraph advertising the inauguration of a new direct air-service between London and a foreign capital. Bring in *one* word from *each* of the seven groups.

1. fashionable—modern—modish—new-fangled—up-to-date
2. comfortable—cosy—luxurious—sensual—snug
3. globe-trotter—passenger—traveller—voyager—wayfarer
4. fast—quick—rapid—speedy—supersonic
5. business man—capitalist—merchant—salesman—trader
6. aeroplane—aircraft—air-liner—plane—vehicle
7. cheap—economical—mean—money-saving—thrifty

Ninety-five

From these 25 sentences, remove the words that are printed in italics. Then rephrase the sentences with the verb 'wish', without changing their meanings in any way. (In some cases, you will have to draw upon your imagination for the new subject.)

Example: 'It is a great pity that you can't come to the sea with us tomorrow.'

Answer: 'We wish you could come to the sea with us tomorrow.'

1. I *am very sorry that* the Smiths are not in town this week-end.
2. *It's a pity that* Mary isn't with us now.
3. He *is sorry that* he makes so many mistakes.
4. *It's a pity that* she has left.
5. *It's a pity that* she left so soon.
6. I *was sorry that* I couldn't accept your invitation.
7. We *are sorry that* we said that to you.
8. *It's a pity that* you smoke so much.
9. *It's a pity that* that restaurant is so dreadfully expensive.
10. I *am sorry that* I must leave you all now.
11. Mary *is sorry that* she was so unkind to Philip.
12. Dr Martin *was sorry that* we had left before he arrived.
13. We *are sorry that* they won't sell us their house.
14. I'*m sorry that* you haven't any time to spare.
15. I *am sorry that* I had to say such a cruel thing.
16. *It's a pity that* I couldn't repair my watch myself.
17. Everybody *is sorry that* Desmond is such an idiot.
18. Roy *is sorry that* he is so absent-minded.
19. *It was a pity that* Rosemary and Arthur didn't get a better seat.
20. I'*m sorry that* I can't speak your language well enough to hold a longer conversation.
21. I *was sorry that* I didn't have anything to give to the poor chap.
22. I'*m sorry that* he burned that particular chair with his cigarette.
23. *It's a pity that* we didn't buy the more expensive ones.
24. I'*m very sorry that* I must now tell you something that will upset you.
25. We'*re sorry that* we haven't anything better than this to offer you.

Ninety-six

Say where the strong stress lies in these 40 words.

Example: recognise
Answer: re<u>c</u>ognise

1. professional	7. beneficial	13. desirable
2. veterinary	8. bequeath	14. collapse
3. intervene	9. temporary	15. blockade
4. benefit	10. celebration	16. apparent
5. celebrate	11. managerial	17. exchange
6. professorial	12. comforting	18. assembly

19. elementary	26. fertile	33. accentuate
20. exercise	27. metaphorical	34. domestic
21. obligation	28. deliberate	35. empire
22. individual	29. medicine	36. incongruous
23. extremity	30. political	37. ambiguity
24. obligatory	31. medicinal	38. domesticity
25. individuality	32. metaphor	39. literary
		40. courageous

Ninety-seven

I don't like it

Rewrite each of the 25 sentences below, including the word or group of words printed on the right-hand side of the vertical line, but making no other change in the sentences. (There may be several correct places for the word or words to be inserted.)

Example: He finished the job.   quickly
Answer: Quickly he finished the job.
He quickly finished the job.
He finished the job quickly.

1. Wasn't he with you?	at the time
2. They're getting married.	next month
3. I don't like it.	very much
4. Supper will be ready.	soon
5. Supper will be ready.	before long
6. He wears a pullover.	seldom
7. She fell heavily.	downstairs
8. The central-heating is on.	full
9. I feel rather worried.	occasionally
10. He's done all this work.	for nothing
11. Paul smokes a cigar.	from time to time
12. He doesn't like this food.	really
13. Everybody enjoyed your party.	enormously
14. I kissed your sister.	only

106

15. I'll have finished this report.	by five o'clock
16. We admire that man.	all
17. They've left the house.	just
18. The postman came here.	just a moment ago
19. She's seen that film.	three times
20. No, we didn't go for a picnic.	last Sunday
21. He was in the Army.	never
22. The car has been polished.	well enough
23. He is late.	always
24. That park is open to the public.	only on weekdays
25. Have you been to the Louvre?	ever

Ninety-eight

In each of these 20 groups of sentences, *one* is incorrect grammatically. Can you say which one it is, and why it is incorrect?

1a. You oughtn't to have said that to her.
 b. You shouldn't have said that to her.
 c. You didn't ought to have said that to her.

2a. Exercise strengthens instead of weakens the body.
 b. Exercise strengthens instead of weakening the body.
 c. Exercise strengthens rather than weakens the body.

3a. Not only did he build a house, he also built a swimming-pool in the garden.
 b. He not only built a house, he built a swimming-pool in the garden, too.
 c. He not only built a house but also a swimming-pool.

4a. Don't be like your brother, wasting time.
 b. Don't waste your time like your brother does.
 c. Don't waste your time as your brother does.

5a. He's a man who I supposed was incapable of such cruelty.
 b. He's a man whom I supposed was incapable of such cruelty.
 c. He's a man whom I supposed to be incapable of such cruelty.

6a. Her new raincoat being so smart, Gwen was impatient for a wet day.
 b. Her new raincoat being such a smart one, Gwen was impatient for a wet day.
 c. Being such a smart new raincoat, Gwen was impatient for a wet day.

7a. It's a long time that I haven't seen her.
 b. It's a long time since I saw her.
 c. I haven't seen her for a long time.

8a. I should like to have been invited to their party.
  b. I should have liked to be invited to their party.
  c. I should have liked to have been invited to their party.

9a. Pamela always goes to the cinema every Monday.
  b. Pamela will always go to the cinema every Monday.
  c. Pamela always uses to go to the cinema every Monday.

10a. If one promises one's wife that one will be home for dinner at eight and one turns up at midnight, one would be wise to bring home a bunch of flowers as well as a good excuse.
  b. If someone promises his wife that he will be home for dinner at eight and he turns up at midnight, he would be wise to bring home a bunch of flowers as well as a good excuse.
  c. If one promises his wife that he will be home for dinner at eight and he turns up at midnight, he would be wise to bring home a bunch of flowers as well as a good excuse.

11a. She ran away rapidly.
  b. She ran away fastly.
  c. She ran away fast.

12a. They put him gently down, after they had carried him for two hours.
  b. They laid him down gently, after carrying him for two hours.
  c. They lay him gently down, after they had carried him for two hours.

13a. Let Peter and I take you there.
  b. Let Peter and me take you there.
  c. Let the two of us take you there.

14a. With this cold of mine I'd better not go out.
  b. I'd better not to go out with this cold of mine.
  c. It'd be better for me not to go out, with this cold of mine.

15a. If Jack were with them last night, he will have given them our message.
  b. If Jack was with them last night, he must have given them our message.
  c. If Jack were with them tomorrow, he would give them our message.

16a. Many of his mistakes were absentminded ones.
  b. Many a mistake of his was absentminded.
  c. Many his mistakes were absentminded.

17a. He was playing a lot of tennis when he was younger.
  b. He used to play a great deal of tennis when he was younger.
  c. He played a good deal of tennis when he was younger.

18a. Need you leave so soon? It's early yet.
  b. Do you need leave so soon? It's still early.
  c. Do you need to leave so soon? It's so early.

19a. They tied him to a tree and whipped him hardly.
  b. They bound him to a tree and beat him cruelly.
  c. They tied him to a tree and flogged him soundly.

20a. Don't these roses smell beautiful?
  b. Don't these roses smell beautifully?
  c. These roses have a beautiful smell, don't you think?

Ninety-nine

In each of these 20 sentences, there are some words printed in italics. Rearrange these words in what seems to you their most usual order.

1. She wore *bright a hat green such* that everybody stared at it in amazement.
2. There was *enough work nearly not* to keep the factory busy.
3. The boy said he would like to have *other the some of toys too*.
4. I'm told that *accident a many tragic* has happened at this corner of the road.
5. They all thought that *of other the green shade* would suit Jane better.
6. That was *the examination by easiest paper far* I have ever seen.
7. We had to attend *the much singing same lessons* every Monday.
8. They live in *stone a new built of red house big*.
9. John thought that twenty miles was *long a far way too* for us to walk.
10. I'm dreadfully sorry to say that I've broken *only the beautiful vase really* in the house.
11. Peter's just told me about *rather a recent hair-raising experience his of* at the airport.
12. He has been ill with measles or *disease such children's some*.
13. No, this wine is *at sweet all too not*.
14. In my new shop I would like to have a stock of groceries and fruit and *very other easily sold any* commodities.
15. We had *there a holiday so wonderful* that we're going again next summer.
16. Whenever he read that story it brought back memories of *his all forgotten but own* childhood.
17. Mary is taking *a time of the devil* reading that book we lent her.
18. Both John and Jane could put the saddle on the horse but John's method was *better much the*.
19. Patricia is *long a chalk by too astute* to have been taken in by that sort of trick.
20. John was late for the meeting because of *things many the other pressing* he had to do.

One hundred

Here is another test of your ability to assimilate the full meaning of something that you read.

What to do:
i. Read each piece once—ONLY ONCE.
ii. Cover the piece in some way, and read the sentences *a, b, c, d* below.[1] Only *one* of these is correct.
iii. Decide which of these four is the correct one. *Do not cheat by looking back at the piece before making your decision.*[2]

1. In the workshop of Mr Jonathan Burge, carpenter and builder, in the village of Hayslope, on the eighteenth of June, 1799, five men were coming to the end of their work for the day, and were looking forward to receiving their just wages.

   a. Five men built the workshop of Mr Jonathan Burge in the village of Hayslope, in 1799.
   b. Mr Jonathan Burge was looking forward to receiving his just wages for his day's work.
   c. Five men would soon be going home.
   d. Mr Jonathan Burge stopped work on the eighteenth of June, 1799.

2. Philip Bracken, seventeen years of age, lost one of his eyes when he was accidentally hit by an airgun pellet in the Birmingham sports-centre recently. The shot was fired by a fellow-athlete, Thomas H. Godlington. Bracken was taken to the County Hospital where he is reported to be in a critical condition.

   a. A Birmingham athlete has been in the County Hospital, in a critical condition, for seventeen days.
   b. One athlete lately shot another in the eye.
   c. The eye was removed at the County Hospital.
   d. The County Hospital is very near the Birmingham sports-centre.

3. The liner 'Agamemnon' changed course two days ago, while sailing in the Aegean Sea, to pick up two seriously injured quarry workers from the island of Carpathos, where there is no hospital. The two men were taken to the island of Rhodes.

   a. Two workers were injured while the ship was changing its course.
   b. The ship took two workers from the island of Rhodes to the island of Carpathos.
   c. It took the ship two days to go from Carpathos to Rhodes.
   d. Carpathos is an island in the Aegean Sea.

---

[1] If you can get somebody to read everything to you, *so that you test your ear too*, the exercise will be even more valuable.
[2] If necessary, see page 14 again for an example.

4. We had such an argument in the family yesterday about what colour the divan covers should be dyed! My wife said it should be brown. Her mother said it should be blue. The children agreed with my wife. I myself thought a darkish green, to tone with the curtains, would be best. In the end, no decision was made.

   a. My children thought the divan covers should be dyed brown.
   b. I thought the curtains should be dyed first.
   c. My mother-in-law agreed with the children.
   d. My wife didn't want to make any decision at all.

5. The Monroes opened their summer place a little late, for carking cares had kept them long in town. The grass was greening and tangled when they arrived, and the house had a woodsy smell. Mr Monroe took a deep breath. 'I'll get a great sleep tonight,' he said. He put on some old clothes, pottered around, inspecting doors and windows, whistling.

   a. When Mr Monroe had put on his old clothes, he had a woodsy smell.
   b. Mr and Mrs Monroe had stayed longer than usual in the city.
   c. Mr Monroe took a deep breath because he liked the woodsy smell.
   d. The Monroes were unable to sleep very well because of carking cares.

6. The policemen went up to him and asked, politely, why he was sitting like that in the middle of the road. He simply grinned up at them, and made no reply. They sighed, nodded at each other, and lifted him forcibly to his feet. As they did so, he began to shout and scream at the top of his voice. In spite of this, the policemen continued to keep their temper under control.

   a. The policemen grinned at the man who was sitting in the road.
   b. The man in the road kept his temper under control as the policemen lifted him forcibly to his feet.
   c. People began to shout at the policemen.
   d. The policemen were surprisingly polite to the man.

7. The clerk of the court said: 'Your name is Peter Frederic Martin, of 26 Jameson Street, W.8?' Martin said: 'It is.' He was leaning with his hands on the front of the dock. As he spoke his Adam's apple shot up and down convulsively in his stringy throat.

   a. The man in the dock was very nervous.
   b. The name of the clerk was Peter Frederic Martin.
   c. Martin was holding an apple in his hands.
   d. The dock was in Jameson Street, W.8.

8. It was in the middle of their sixth dance that she felt him stiffen. She looked up at him and saw he was staring at the door. Five burly

men in dark suits were standing just inside the entrance, staring in their direction. She felt herself grow cold. 'What is it?' she breathed. 'They look like policemen.'

a. He saw that she was staring at the door.
b. He had already danced with her five times.
c. Standing inside the entrance, she felt cold.
d. Standing inside the entrance, he felt cold.

9. Blore was sitting with cool immobility in the far corner of the tent at a small table of teakwood, writing with spectacled eyes held at a careful distance from the page. There was a singular absence of heroism in him. To Forrester, he looked less like an officer than a sort of cart-horse. But it was too hot to say so.

a. Blore thought that Forester looked like a cart-horse.
b. Forrester was not a heroic type.
c. There is a singular absence of heroism about a cart-horse.
d. Blore was sitting some distance away from Forrester.

10. In a hot railway carriage there were two small girls and a small boy in the care of their aunt, and a bachelor who was sitting as far away from them as possible. The children were bored with the journey, and were consequently troublesome. Most of the aunt's remarks began with 'Don't', and nearly all of the children's began with 'Why?'.

a. The aunt told the bachelor not to sit so far away from the children.
b. The children wanted to know why the bachelor was sitting so far away from them.
c. The children were tired of the journey.
d. Everybody was troubled by the heat of the railway carriage.